MORE LAST DAYS OF STEAM IN

HAMPSHIRE

AND THE ISLE OF WIGHT

Running light engine past the allotments to the west of Cosham on 4.3.60, the long front overhang and stovepipe chimney of 0–6–0 No. 30692 typify the unmistakable characteristics of a Drummond class 700 'Black Motor'. Built by Dubs in 1897, the entire class of thirty survived well into British Railways days after being superheated in the twenties.

More Last Days of Steam in
HAMPSHIRE
and the Isle of Wight

—D. FEREDAY GLENN—

ALAN SUTTON

First published in the United Kingdom in 1993 by
Alan Sutton Publishing Ltd · Phoenix Mill · Stroud · Gloucestershire

First published in the United States of America in 1993 by
Alan Sutton Publishing Inc · 83 Washington Street · Dover · NH 03820

British Library Cataloguing in Publication Data

Glenn, David Fereday
More Last Days of Steam in Hampshire and
the Isle of Wight
I. Title
385.09422

ISBN 0–7509–0224–8

Library of Congress Cataloging in Publication Data

Glenn, D.F. (David Fereday)
    More last days of steam in Hampshire and the Isle of Wight / D. Fereday Glenn
    ISBN 0-7509-0224-8: $ 29.00
1. Locomotives- - England- - Hampshire. 2. Railroads- - England- - Hampshire.
3. Locomotives- - England- - Isle of Wight. 4. Railroads- - England- - Isle of Wight. I. Title
TJ603.4.G7H3624 1993
385'. 09422'7- - dc20   92-40836
                                                                                        CIP

Jacket photographs: front: Southampton survivor: The 1893-built Corrall Queen *(alias Adams B4 0–4–0T No. 30096) shuffles past Northam Gasworks with some coal wagons bound for Dibles Wharf one spring day in March 1968. Once named* Normandy *it spent many years shunting in the Eastern Docks – where Ocean Village now stands; back: Military midsummer: LMR 0–6–0ST No. 195 crosses a rural byway as it leaves Liss Forest Road station on 30.6.67. The single carriage train was used by civilian employees at Longmoor Camp as well as military personnel of the Royal Corps of Transport until closure in late 1969. Endpapers: front: One of the diminutive Drummond C14 0–4–0Ts, No. 30588, painted in fully-lined out secondary passenger livery, poses with an Adams class B4 0–4–0T at the rear of Eastleigh MPD on 18.2.56; back: Namesake of the class N15 series of 4–6–0s renowned for their exploits on the West of England main line, No. 30453* King Arthur *stands forlorn on the scrap road at Eastleigh (71A) on 27. 7. 61.*

All photographs by the author unless otherwise stated.

Typeset in 9/10 Palatino.
Typesetting and origination by
Alan Sutton Publishing Limited.
Printed and bound in Great Britain by
WBC, Bridgend, Mid Glam.

Introduction

To business that we love we rise betime,
And go to't with delight.

So Shakespeare wrote, and I cannot think of a better way to describe the simple pleasure of putting together a further volume about the railways of my native county. As I write this, it is just a quarter of a century since steam breathed its last on the Southern Region of British Railways: sheds at Eastleigh, Bournemouth and just across the county boundary at Salisbury fell silent to the sights and sounds of the steam age from 10 July 1967. Here and there around the margins one or two survivors worked on, periodically, for a year or two under other management – at Corralls on Dibles Wharf in Southampton, or under military discipline at Marchwood or Longmoor – but elsewhere it seemed the fires had gone out all over Hampshire and in the Isle of Wight for the last time.

It is difficult to describe now, to younger generations who have grown up to the thrill of steam revived under preservation, the magic of those same engines (and their vanished fellows) in the grimy, shabby fifties and sixties. To unbelievers and those born too late to know what the railways were like during the first twenty years of Nationalization it must seem strange, this hankering after the past. Yet, without any disrespect to the monumental achievements of preservation, the harsh, dirty and increasingly decrepit reality of the years between 1948 and 1967 was a kind of 'Golden Age' that will never come again. Throughout the period, the relentless catalogue of closures and withdrawals served only to intensify one's interest in what was left, until the dread realization that the battle was lost. It is a measure of the tenacity and perseverance of groups and individuals, who, since 1967, have endeavoured to secure a future for steam not just in Hampshire and the Isle of Wight but all over the country, that almost all the hulks that rusted in a South Wales scrap-yard for years have been recovered; many have seen active service again, while others are pursuing the tortuous path to the same goal. A few years ago two former Southern locomotives were repatriated from the New World, both to resume haulage of trains in their respective spheres – a feat few would have believed possible back in the sixties. But it *is* different today. Once mankind had achieved the 'impossible' by landing on the moon (and coming back!), the boundaries of human endeavour were enlarged accordingly. The war has been won.

Those who may not have read any of my previous books might wonder how I, a vintage-bus preservationist, came to have such an interest in railways. As a small child in the 1940s I used to wait on the foot-bridge at Cosham whenever a train was signalled, watching in awe as the smoke was blasted between the wooden planks by the fiery monster beneath. Though I did not harbour any secret ambition to be an engine driver, as a student I was sorely tempted to part-own a little 'OF' 0–4–0ST discovered still at work in Goole Docks in 1960 – the sum quoted by British Railways for the 'wee Pug' was very modest, even then, but there was the proverbial problem of where to keep a 21 ton locomotive! As two other examples of the same series have been saved, I have no regrets at

At the south end of Fareham station an imposing gantry of signals controlled the exit from platform 2: left for Portchester, Cosham, Havant or Portsmouth, right for Fort Brockhurst and Gosport. Smaller repeater arms were mounted at eye-level for the benefit of locomotive crews stopped in the station, while the topmost arms could be seen above the foot-bridge by foot-platemen approaching from the north. In this July 1955 view, class K 2–6–0 No. 32349 enters platform 3 with a Fratton – Salisbury freight.

not pursuing the matter. But since then twenty-five years' involvement with, and restoration of, traditional coach-built motor buses has instilled the most profound respect for those who give up their time for steam.

One of the difficulties for school children and students in my era was a lack of mobility; a bicycle was essential for any kind of social life, as well as fundamental for serious train spotting! It would be perfectly feasible to put together an album of railway pictures entitled *Last Days of Steam around Fareham*, simply because it has been my home since 1948. In deference to the publisher and the interests of a wider public, however, that approach has been eschewed! Instead, Fareham is but one of the main railway centres covered in the broader context of Hampshire. But I do have a very tangible remnant, from that station, of bygone days, in the shape of a lower-quadrant signal arm and spectacle plate that used to dominate the junction at the south end until 1956, controlling admission to the Gosport line from platform 2. It remains a wonder that it did not get broken (like all the others) during its descent from the top of the gantry, but fifty-odd years up there in all weathers must have made it tough. Sold by Waterloo for the sum of 5s. (25p) and borne home in triumph spread-eagled on my bicycle – a task that took almost two hours for a distance of 1½ miles – the old semaphore is still in 'as withdrawn' condition besmirched with soot from the age of steam.

As usual, I am grateful to Margaret Lovell for her valuable second opinion in the matter of picture selection and help with proof-reading. I am also indebted to those other photographers whose pictures have helped to broaden coverage of railways in Hampshire and the Isle of Wight. If the book gives readers as much pleasure as its preparation has given me, it will have served its purpose well.

David Fereday Glenn

MORE LAST DAYS OF STEAM IN

HAMPSHIRE

AND THE ISLE OF WIGHT

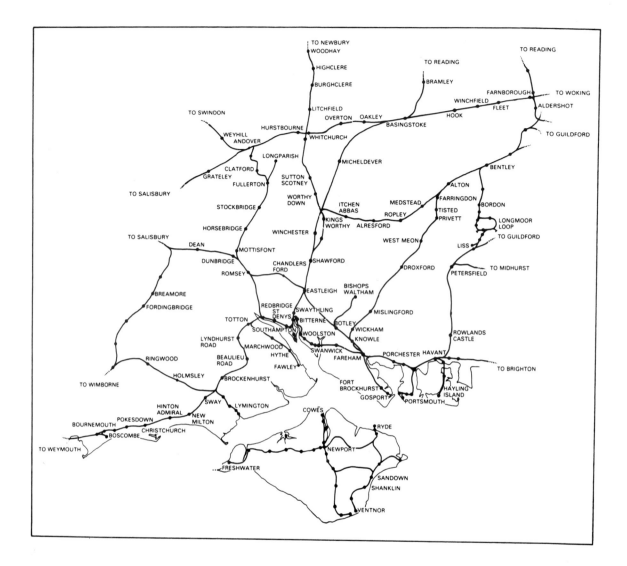

Mainland Locomotive Depots

As the smallest of the six Regions established under the newly-nationalized British Railways in 1948, the Southern had but a handful of steam Motive Power Depots within Hampshire and the Isle of Wight. For the purpose of this book, Hampshire will be taken to include Bournemouth and Christchurch, etc., for such places only became part of East Dorset after the re-organization of local government and county boundaries in 1974 – several years after the official end of steam traction on BR. And, because it provided loco-motives for many diagrams within Hampshire, both south-eastward to Romsey, Southampton (or Eastleigh) and Portsmouth as well as south to Fordingbridge and Bournemouth, Salisbury shed is being incorporated too.

The full list of MPDs extant in 1951 – the year of publication of the oldest complete Ian Allan *Loco-Shed Book* in my possession – shows the following depots and sub-sheds:

70D	Basingstoke
71A	EASTLEIGH (with sub-sheds at Winchester (City), Lymington (Town) and Andover Junction)
71B	Bournemouth (Central)
71D	Fratton (with sub-sheds at Gosport and Midhurst)
71E	Newport ⎫
71F	Ryde (St Johns) ⎬ Isle of Wight
71G	Branksome (as sub-shed of Bath, Somerset & Dorset line)
71I	Southampton Docks
72B	Salisbury

In later years Fratton became 70F, Newport 70G and Ryde 70H; likewise Branksome became a sub-shed of Bournemouth (71B) rather than Bath.

As steam locomotives were withdrawn and rail services suspended or converted for diesel or electric operation, this list of MPDs shrank. Fratton roundhouse, for example, was used for the storage of some historic locomotives destined for the National Collection in the 1960s, while turning facilities and coaling remained available almost until the eclipse of steam. But, as is well known, many of those that ended up in Barry yard in South Wales were salvaged for restoration; a few have even returned to active use on special excursions over BR tracks, most recently the rebuilt 'West Country' No. 34027 *Taw Valley* from Waterloo to Southampton and Bournemouth some twenty-five years after the type was ousted by electrification!

In a biting wind, veteran Drummond 'Black Motor' 0–6–0 No. 30316 stands at the north end of Eastleigh shed, snow-plough at the ready, on 18.1.58. Several of the 700 class engines had their front buffer-beams drilled for the mounting of snow-ploughs, but fortunately the need to use them seldom arose. Note the upturned chimney on the ash alongside the tender.

Fresh from overhaul, auto-fitted class M7 0–4–4T No. 30050 was in light steam at the south end of Eastleigh shed on 30.4.61. Only long-framed (formerly X14) examples were converted to push-pull operation, as only they had sufficient space for the reservoir to be mounted below the front buffer-beam. In this view No. 30050 is coupled to similar engine No. 30328; both worked for a time after 1949 on the Petersfield–Midhurst–Pulborough branch services.

Built by Neilson in 1883 to Adams' design, class 0395 0–6–0 No. 30575 (SR No. 3439) was nearing the end of its long working life when it appeared at 71A on 16.2.57. All these elderly locomotives were withdrawn by 1959. In the background of the picture can be seen some of the railwaymen's cottages that front onto Campbell Road, between the works and the shed.

The 'scrap road' was likely to be the last resting place for the majority of steam engines, large and small. On 11.11.56 one of the smaller examples stored at Eastleigh was Adams class O2 0–4–4T No. 30223. Most of the O2s retained their Adams boilers, but a handful of Drummond boilers rotated among the survivors – and 30223 had one of these. Note the sacking over the chimney, to minimize corrosion.

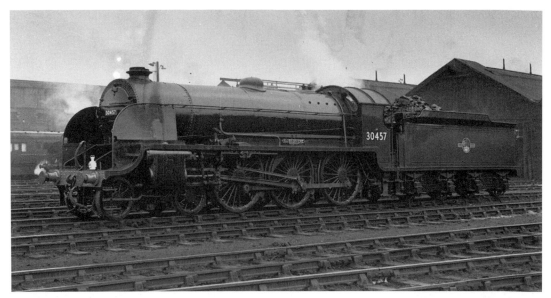

Last of the 'Eastleigh Arthurs' to have a full overhaul, class N15 4–6–0 No. 30457 *Sir Bedivere* looks immaculate as it simmers at the north end of the shed on 22.3.59. Several of this series were coupled to older-style ex-LSWR bogie tenders for Salisbury–Exeter duties, but *Sir Bedivere* was not one of them.

Waiting its turn to be coaled-up, Fairburn 4MT 2–6–4T No. 42067 appears to have been running-in after overhaul at Eastleigh Works as the shedplate shows 75A (Brighton). At this date, 18.2.56, a number of this LMS-designed class remained at work on the Southern, mostly in Kent and Sussex, but during 1957/8 they were exchanged for BR Standard 4 tanks numbered in the 80xxx series.

Some impression of the sheer number of steam locomotives that could be seen on shed at Eastleigh before the influx of diesels can be glimpsed in this picture. Exiled from its native London area – it was formerly based at Hither Green (73C) – class W 2–6–4T No. 31916 had the task of positioning other engines around the depot. The three cylinder W tanks were prohibited from working passenger trains, so their main function at Eastleigh was on oil trains to and from Fawley Refinery. The date was 27.7.61.

From 1956 onwards there was a steady procession of rebuilt Bulleid Pacific locomotives arriving on shed from the works. 'Merchant Navy' class 4–6–2 No. 35005 *Canadian Pacific* had its air-smoothed casing removed and chain-driven valve gear replaced by Walschaerts motion during May 1959; it appeared resplendent in its new guise on 7.6.59. This same locomotive is today restored to full working order at Loughborough on the Great Central line.

Nominally a rebuild of Drummond's solitary E14 4–6–0 No. 335 (built 1907), the engine that Urie produced in 1914 was almost completely new, although it carried the same stock number. The tender had come from Drummond's double-single loco (class T7 No. 720) due to excessive water consumption! As reincarnated by Urie, the engine lingered on at Salisbury shed performing local passenger and freight haulage reclassified as H15. As No. 30335 it stood on the scrap line at Eastleigh on 7.6.59.

The shapely lines of a Billinton ex-LBSCR 2–6–0 were not entirely out of place at the cradle of former LSWR motive power, as two of the seventeen K class locomotives regularly worked the 10.03 a.m. Eastleigh–Fratton Yard freight for years. No. 32344 made an appearance at the shed on 9.6.61, after some attention to the smokebox and front end. Sadly, the entire class was withdrawn in 1962.

Many former LSWR locomotives went for scrap in 1961. One of the last of Adams class G6 0–6–0T design to remain in traffic was No. 30258 of Basingstoke, but by 27.7.61 it had been towed to Eastleigh. The 1894-built engine stood with a withdrawn T9 4–4–0 amid heaps of coal in the shed yard.

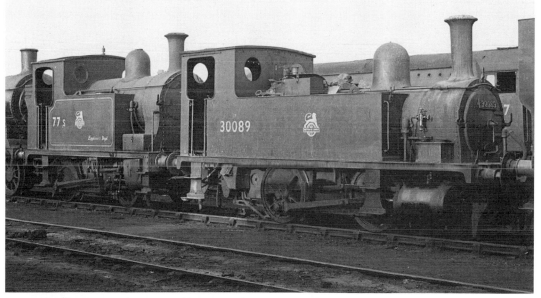

On St David's Day 1959 the afternoon sunshine illuminated a pair of four-coupled survivors. The older of the two was class B4 No. 30089, built in 1892 and formerly named *Trouville*, while the smaller engine was the last Drummond C14 class 77s (SR No. 0745). The little C14 was withdrawn and scrapped within days, but the B4 was transferred to Guildford as shed pilot for several more years.

Western Region engines were relatively infrequent visitors to Eastleigh shed, though they passed through the station daily on Newbury line trains or Reading–Portsmouth duties. On 18.8.57 Churchward 2–6–0 No. 5369, then based at 84E (Tyseley), was out of steam at the north end of the shed. Note the breakdown crane alongside.

Rare bird: former Plymouth, Devonport & South Western Junction Railway 0–6–2T No. 30757 *Earl of Mount Edgcumbe* retired from its native West Country in 1956, but was used for shunting at Eastleigh for some months before final withdrawal. Built by Hawthorn Leslie in 1907, it had 4 ft 0 in driving wheels and a minute coal bunker. Waiting its turn to take on more fuel, 30757 was in light steam in front of the sludge tower on 29.12.56.

In total contrast to most other occupants of the shed on 9.3.62, the sole surviving Drummond class T9 'Greyhound' 4–4–0, No. 120, was spotless after overhaul in the works. Painted in LSWR green, with black and white lining and fitted with chimney capuchon typical of early-1920s condition, this engine gave delight to many by hauling special passenger trains for a period of about eighteen months at locations throughout the Southern Region, before being put into store for the National Collection. In the 1980s it was restored to traffic on the Watercress line, first in BR lined black condition as No. 30120 and later as SR No. 120 in the olive green livery of the 1930s; it is now based at Swanage and will be given a further overhaul to return it to full mainline specification.

Visits to the works, which had been constructed in Dugald Drummond's time to replace the one at Nine Elms, were a special privilege. On 9.2.57 one of the oldest surviving LSWR locomotives, Beattie 2–4–0WT No. 30586 of 1875, was receiving a major overhaul. Of the three well tanks remaining in stock, 30586 was unique in having rectangular driving wheel splashers; it lasted until 1962, based at Wadebridge in North Cornwall.

At the works open day on 7.8.57 three class 8F 2–8–0 locomotives were to be seen. Numbered 48773–5, they were formerly War Department stock in the Canal Zone but repatriated in the 1950s and based on the Longmoor Military Railway; they were transferred to BR in 1957 and overhauled at Eastleigh prior to entering service with the LM Region. No. 48774 is pictured looking very smart but without a smokebox door number-plate.

Much of Bournemouth's steam locomotive allocation – and visiting engines – could be viewed from the platforms of Central station. One of the visitors on 9.1.57 was 'Greyhound' No. 30313, awaiting its opportunity to set off tender-first for the West station to power a stopping passenger train to Salisbury. This T9 4–4–0 was one of the 1900-built batch with full-width cab and splashers, while the six-wheel tender was received when transferred on loan to the Eastern Section lines (which had small turntables) between 1924 and 1940. Note the old van body used as a store shed.

For a brief period in 1959 a small number of ex-SECR 4–4–0s rebuilt by Maunsell were tried on Salisbury–Bournemouth local services as replacements for withdrawn 'Greyhounds'. Class E1 No. 31507 was to be found on the short spur beyond the turntable at Bournemouth on 8.11.59. Perhaps the newcomers were not in the best of condition, or maybe the innate conservatism of South Western crews meant the trials were unpopular; whatever the reason, the Chatham engines did not stay long and were replaced by Standard class 4s.

A Riddles Standard design that became much associated with the Bournemouth and Weymouth services until the end of steam on the Southern was the class 5 4–6–0. Several were also allocated to the Somerset & Dorset line, appearing on 'The Pines Express' from the mid-1950s. No. 73118 was in the shed yard beside Central station on 9.1.57 – note the 'Quiet Please' injunction to enginemen! Not long afterwards, 73118 took over the name *King Leodegrance* from withdrawn N15 No. 30739.

Until 1957 the handsome Marsh Atlantics of the former LBSCR made occasional visits to Bournemouth at the head of the 9.40 a.m. through service from Brighton. On the morning of 16.1.57 the last class H2 4–4–2, No. 32424 *Beachy Head*, brought the train from Brighton into Bournemouth Central station, then uncoupled and ran forward to be turned and coaled, etc. in the shed yard, ready for the return journey during the afternoon. *Beachy Head* was the only remaining Atlantic active in the United Kingdom at that time.

From the long 'Down' platform at Bournemouth Central there was a splendid panorama of the Motive Power Depot. On 17.10.66 the occupants included a Standard 4 2–6–4T, rebuilt 'West Country' 4–6–2 No. 34093 (formerly *Saunton*) and Riddles 4MT 2–6–0 No. 76026. Another 2–6–4T, No. 80134, was passing by on the 'Up' through line, light engine.

The two-road structure at Branksome, in the triangle of lines outside Bournemouth West station, was used by Somerset & Dorset engines. Formerly a sub-shed of Bath (71G), it later became a sub-shed of Bournemouth (71B). On 6.8.55, a typical summer Saturday, Branksome was quite busy with visiting locomotives on through holiday trains from the Midlands and the North that had been routed over the S & D. In the background can be discerned a Stanier 'Black 5' 4–6–0, a class often employed until Standard 4s and 5s took over, while in the foreground stands a Fowler class 2P 4–4–0 built in 1928. No. 40569 arrived on a stopping train from Templecombe, where it was shedded (71H).

After turning on the triangle past the electric carriage sheds, Eastleigh-based class H15 4–6–0 No. 30474 simmers beside the roundhouse at Fratton on 27.11.59. The weekday empty stock train from Fratton Yard generally required a powerful 4–6–0, for the load could run to fifteen bogies or more – a task well suited to the Urie or Maunsell engines of classes H15, N15 or S15. For some inexplicable reason the H15 series became extinct first.

The last operational 'Terrier' 0–6–0T to retain its original smokebox was the Lancing Carriage Works shunter, DS680. It was discovered inside Fratton roundhouse – partially dismantled – on 1.4.61; perhaps it suffered a hot-box while on route for Eastleigh Works. Still classified as A1, rather than A1x, the former LBSCR No. 654 was built in 1875 and is now preserved in Canada as No. 54 *Waddon*.

By 1961 Fratton had ceased to have its own allocation and became a sub-shed under Eastleigh. On 29.9.61 one of the regular performers on the Hayling branch was shunting coal wagons outside the roundhouse: this study of class A1x 0–6–0T No. 32661 shows the spark-arrestor fitted to the tall chimney, and its small size when compared to the standard 16T mineral wagon behind. No. 32661 retained its small bunker because it was not one of the class that worked in the Isle of Wight (where bunkers were enlarged) and, while most of the survivors of this fifty-strong class found new homes in preservation, this engine was not so fortunate.

By the ash pits and coaling crane, two representatives of the former 'Brighton' line stood alongside each other on 26.8.58. No. 32139 was one of the elderly Stroudley class E1 0–6–0Ts, while No. 32479 was an 0–6–2T of class E4. The former type was employed shunting at Fratton Yard or on short trip workings to HM Dockyard, whereas the 0–6–2T might be used for carriage shunting or with through coaches on the occasional passenger train to or from Fareham.

Fratton shed sustained a direct hit in the bombing of Portsmouth during the Second World War, but repairs were effected and the roundhouse continued to be used regularly until the end of the 1950s. On 1.7.60 the depot was empty except for a solitary Maunsell class L1 4–4–0 in store. No. 31757 remained at Fratton for several years but was never steamed again; none of this class has been preserved.

The three-cylinder Maunsell 2–6–0s of class U1 had sometimes worked passenger trains into Portsmouth prior to electrification in the late 1930s, but were not often seen there in subsequent years. A pre-Christmas appearance at Fratton by No. 31907 on 23.12.59 was most likely due to it being rostered for one of the many extra mail and parcels duties at that time of year. In company with various other 2–6–0s it stood outside the shed with the fire banked up, a keen north-westerly wind whipping the smoke away from the chimney in the winter sunshine.

The three-road shed was in the Old (or Eastern) Docks. It had been the home of the Adams class B4 0–4–0T engines from the 1890s until 1947, when their duties were taken over by fourteen of the US Transportation Corps shunters, suitably modified. By the 1960s one of the surviving B4 tanks was once more engaged in the docks: on 14.1.61 No. 30102 pauses by the roadside in front of the depot, while USA 0–6–0T No. 30070 gets up steam in the background.

The distinctive outline of the USA class 0–6–0T was associated with Southampton Docks through-out the BR steam era, fourteen being purchased after the war. On 7.4.63 several were on shed, as it was a Sunday, the overhead water cranes being clearly discernible. The entire class was equipped with two-way radio, aerials being mounted at the front of both side tanks. No. 30067 also exhibited duty disc 9 and two sets of three-link couplings on the front buffer-team.

Salisbury was another place where Southern and Western Region locomotives might be seen on shed together. Coal trains from South Wales brought eight-coupled engines – both tender and tank variants – while cross-country services from Brighton resulted in engine-changing activities there. On 29.10.55 Churchward 2–8–0 No. 2870, base at Aberdare (86J), was about to leave 72B depot to back down to the yard, where it was due to head the 3.10 p.m. freight for Severn Tunnel junction. In the background 'West Country' class 4–6–2 No. 34047 *Callington* waited to return to Brighton (75A) with the through train from Plymouth.

After a prolonged wet spell the puddles by the coaling stage at Salisbury were like a miniature lake. Maunsell class Z 0–8–0T No. 30957 is reflected in the water for a moment or two as it shuffles past on 4.10.58, facing toward the west. The substantial brick-built engine shed can be seen beyond. There were only eight Z tanks, designed for heavy shunting, and 30957 was allocated to 72B for a number of years before moving further west to Exmouth junction (72A).

The vast bulk of WR 2–8–2T No. 7202 occupied most of the turntable at Salisbury on 4.10.58. Weighing in at 92 tons, the engine was rebuilt from a Churchward 2–8–0T in 1934 with an extended bunker to give it a greater range. After turning, 7202 was due to head a freight to Severn Tunnel junction and thence return to its home at Radyr (88A). This engine was rescued from Barry scrapyard and is to be restored at Didcot to full working order.

Isle of Wight Interlude

Departure for the Isle of Wight is from the berth at the seaward end of Portsmouth Harbour station. On 25.7.61 the car ferry *Wootton* was moored in mid-channel, while PS *Ryde* steamed past the submarine base (HMS *Dolphin*) to form the 9.50 a.m. sailing from Clarence Pier to Ryde via South Parade Pier. While principal sailings between Portsmouth and Ryde (Pier Head) appeared in table 50 of the Southern Region timetable, the full steamer services were shown in tables 57 and 57A.

With the steam heating working well, class 02 0–4–4T No. W22 *Brading* makes a lively exit from platform 1 on 28.1.65 in charge of a Ryde Pier Head–Ventnor service. With their 4 ft 10 in driving wheels, these elderly four-coupled engines were ideal for the short but undulating journeys on island routes – hence their survival until the end of steam on 31.12.66.

Almost a full house at Ryde Pier Head on 3.10.65: the Ventnor train was taking water in platform 1 while a service train for Newport and Cowes stood ready to go at platform 2, an enthusiasts' special being already signalled in platform 4. All were headed by vintage class 02 0–4–4T locomotives designed by William Adams for the LSWR and brought over to the island after the Grouping. From left to right the numbers were W24 (formerly *Calbourne*), W26 *Whitwell* and W28 *Ashey*. The tracks of the pier tramway, also owned by British Railways, can be seen in the foreground.

In the final year, 02 No. W20 *Shanklin* emits steam from various parts of its anatomy as it restarts a Pier Head–Ventnor train from Ryde Esplanade station on 17.2.66. All carriages were pre-Grouping in origin so, in company with the nineteenth-century motive power, the entire island system gave the impression of a relic from the Edwardian period – a working 'museum railway'.

By the 1960s, Ryde depot had been given the code 70H. On 27.3.64 neither of the class 02 0–4–4Ts in this view exhibited shedplates, though both still retained their cast name-plates. W30 (in front of the shed) was named *Shorwell* while W36 (nearest the camera) carried the name *Carisbrooke*. W35/36 were the last 02s to be delivered to the island, arriving in 1949 as replacements for the two remaining 'Terrier' 0–6–0T locos.

If passenger trains on the island seemed old-fashioned, the freight wagons were archaic. In the summer of 1963 class 02 0–4–4T W33 *Bembridge* manfully tackled a lengthy load of ancient four-wheeled wagons of various kinds, including no less than *three* brake vans, bound for Newport. *Bembridge* was recorded pounding away from Ryde St John's towards Smallbrook junction, crossing over from the 'Up line past the works headshunt.

Inside the depot at Ryde St John's on 13.8.59, the last island 0–6–0T – class E1 No. W4 *Wroxall* – was out of steam, still with its Newport (70G) shedplate. Transferred from the mainland in 1933 (where it had been numbered B131), it joined three more Stroudley E1s for goods and excursion traffic, surviving until 1961. After the withdrawal of *Wroxall*, all passenger and goods trains on the Isle of Wight were worked by 02 0–4–4T engines.

In high summer island engines sometimes exhibited duty numbers to assist signalmen and other railway staff to recognize the particular train approaching – a modest imitation of the GWR/WR use of reporting numbers, perhaps. On 6.7.60 class O2 0–4–4T W16 *Ventnor* was bound for Newport and Cowes, displaying duty disc No. 10 as it gathered pace restarting from Ryde St John's with the usual rake of non-corridor pre-Grouping stock.

Gleaming after attention from the cleaners, a brace of elderly O2 0–4–4Ts pause at Ryde St John's with the LCGB special to Ventnor on 3.10.65. With W24 (formerly *Calbourne*) coupled ahead of W14 *Fishbourne* (built in 1889), the six-coach train was well within their capacity. As it was no longer the peak summer season, Smallbrook junction box had been closed for the winter and the full complement of signal arms restored to the gantry controlling the 'Down' platform and bay.

With smoke and steam from the chimney casting a shadow over the front of the engine, W33 *Bembridge* blasts out of Brading station at the head of a Ryde to Ventnor service on 26.9.65. Until September 1953 Brading had been the junction station for the branch to St Helens and Bembridge. The class 02 0–4–4T *Bembridge* stayed at work until the end of steam on the island on 31.12.66; it had been built for the LSWR as No. 218 in 1892.

On a perfect summer day, class 02 0–4–4T No. W21 *Sandown* gets a clear road and draws briskly away from the 'Down' platform at Shanklin with a Ryde–Ventnor train on 25.7.61. Even before the end of steam, services terminated at Shanklin from 18.4.66, thus leaving just $8^{1}/_{2}$ miles of the Isle of Wight railway network to electrify.

Busy moment at Wroxall: 'Up' and 'Down' trains used to pass twice per hour at the height of the summer. In this view, probably recorded during the last peak season in 1965, 02 0–4–4T W16 *Ventnor* was arriving with a Ventnor-bound service while a train for Ryde was obliged to wait for the single line to be cleared before proceeding towards Shanklin. Wroxall and Ventnor stations were closed from 18.4.66, thus depriving holiday-makers of a through service by train; a substitute bus operated from Shanklin.

The News, Portsmouth

Ventnor station was intended for closure at the end of the summer of 1965, but was reprieved until the following spring. On 3.10.65 one of the stalwart 02s, W28 *Ashey*, stands at the terminus immediately after arrival from Ryde Pier Head with steam leaking in all directions after its exertions. Note the steep sides of the cutting below St Boniface Down.

Oldest of the IOW class 02 0–4–4Ts, W14 *Fishbourne* was well burnished for its appearance on the LCGB special on 3.10.65. Still fully lined-out and with neat brass name-plate attached on the tankside, the 1889-built veteran was coupled to classmate W24 (formerly *Calbourne*, painted in unlined black) at Ventnor station, safety valves lifting in readiness for the return journey to Ryde. For many years *Fishbourne* was associated with the Brading to Bembridge branch, until its closure in September 1953.

Only days before total closure, 02 0–4–4T No. W24 (formerly named *Calbourne*) storms out of Newport with a Ryde–Cowes service. Over the years since Nationalization what had once been a busy station with four platforms and three different routes was about to disappear off the railway map. W24 was the last 02 to receive a general overhaul at Ryde Works, emerging in plain black without its name-plates, but today it is preserved on the Isle of Wight Steam Railway at Haven Street. This was the scene on 17.2.66.

On a cold, bright winter's day, echoes rang around the station as W18 *Ningwood* blasted away from Ashey with a three-coach train for Newport and Cowes on 28.1.65. When the original Ashey station became unsafe, a new simple platform and brick shelter were constructed on the opposite side of the single line. Now occasional steam trains run through between Smallbrook junction and Wootton but, as yet, stop only at Haven Street on the preserved Isle of Wight Steam Railway.

Beneath the station canopy, class 02 0–4-4T W24 comes to rest at Cowes with an afternoon train from Ryde (Pier Head) on 26.9.65. The shadow of closure was hanging over the line from Smallbrook junction, but this was delayed until February 1966. Although a run-round loop was provided, the four carriages were 'fly-shunted' into a siding and then allowed to run back into the platform with the guard applying the handbrake.

The end of the line: with the 'Down' platform blocked off in connection with winter repairs and coming electrification, on the last day of steam services trains had to use the 'Up' platform at Ryde Esplanade for both arrivals and departures. On 31.12.66 class 02 0–4–4T W27 *Merstone* made one of its final revenue-earning journeys with a stately exit at the head of a train to Shanklin as the short winter's day drew to a close. It was steamed just once more, to tow other withdrawn 02s to the scrap siding at Newport, in April 1967.

Over the sea to Ryde. . . . Out in the Solent, pre-war and post-war vessels of the Southern Railway pass between Portsmouth and Ryde Pier Head, both then owned by British Railways (Southern Region). Last of the 'paddlers', PS *Ryde* survived until 1970 in its traditional role, while MV *Southsea* was displaced from the Solent by smaller, faster catamarans in the 1980s.

Around Bournemouth

The rural peace of Verwood was not unduly disturbed by the arrival of the Saturdays only 1.12 p.m. Salisbury–Bournemouth West service on 25.7.59. Class T9 4–4–0 No. 30707 drifted in with a Maunsell corridor set, to await the arrival from the south of the 1.20 p.m from Bournemouth West in the loop. This cross-country route closed after 4.5.64.

Even the power of 'King Arthur' class 4–6–0 No. 30773 *Sir Lavaine* was checked somewhat by the daunting 1 in 75 gradient of Broadstone bank, as it neared the summit with the 5.05 p.m. stopping service from Southampton Terminus to Wimborne on 18.4.60. The route from Brockenhurst was via Sway, Christchurch and Bournemouth Central.

On the Saturday of August Bank Holiday weekend (2.8.58) the 10.30 a.m. Salisbury–Bournemouth West stopping train was loaded to eight bogies. 'Greyhound' 4–4–0 No. 30120 gave its best shot and staggered up the gruelling 1 in 60 of Parkstone bank with some very assorted stock behind the tender. Poole gasworks dominates the skyline.

Beneath the graceful three-arch bridge, class 4F 0–6–0 No. 44135 plods up Parkstone bank on 17.5.59 with the Whit Sunday excursion from Weston-super-Mare to Bournemouth West. The route had been over the Highbridge branch to Evercreech Junction, then via Templecombe (Lower) to Broadstone junction and Poole – normally no trains ran over the Highbridge line on Sundays.

Bournemouth Central station in the last days of steam traction: an almost anonymous Bulleid Pacific stands at the 'Up' main platform after taking water with a service for London (Waterloo). Bereft of name-plates and front number-plate, it is impossible to distinguish which locomotive it might be from the 'Down' platform (contemporary notes show it must have been 'West Country' No. 34012, formerly named *Launceston*). The bogie van behind the tender, semaphore signalling and 1885 station building are noteworthy.

Still steam-hauled but without a headboard, the 'Bournemouth Belle' arrives at Bournemouth Central station with rebuilt 'West Country' 4–6–2 No. 34040 *Crewkerne* in charge on 17.10.66. In the background the South Western Hotel looms on the skyline. Electric trains were running within nine months.

Unusual motive power for the 'Bournemouth Belle'; some three-quarters of an hour late, perhaps due to engine failure and substitution, the all-Pullman train swept round the curve from Gasworks junction for the final mile into the West station behind class N15 4–6–0 No. 30773 *Sir Lavaine*. This occurred on Sunday, 8.2.59; today there is no 'Belle' and the section of track between Gasworks junction and Bournemouth West junction has been lifted, while the West station closed from 4.10.65.

Before the opening, in 1888, of the direct route from Brockenhurst to Bournemouth via Sway, Christchurch had a rail service via Ringwood and Hurn from 1862. This very traditional train of green corridor stock hauled by Standard class 5 4–6–0 No. 73085 almost conceals the presence of a third (conductor) rail alongside the track, but not quite; the date was 17.10.66. With exhaust shooting skywards, the powerful Riddles design had an easy task with a stopping service to Bournemouth Central only months before the whole operation was taken over by soulless electric multiple units.

Around Brockenhurst, and the Lymington branch

The 'Old Road', the original 1847 Castleman's Corkscrew route from Brockenhurst, was severed between Lymington junction and Ringwood from 4.5.64 following withdrawal of the passenger services to West Moors and Wimborne. Ringwood remained open for freight for a time, but a final special passenger train was run from the Bournemouth area (originating in London) on 16.10.66. Chimney to chimney, Standard class 3 No. 77014 and class 4 2–6–0 No. 76026 shuffle over the level crossing at Ashley Heath Halt on their way to Ringwood, double track still being in place throughout.

A Bournemouth–Waterloo express accelerates steadily away from the 'Up' platform at Brockenhurst on a crisp spring day in the last few years of steam on this route. One of the oldest of Bulleid's 'Light Pacific' locomotives, 'West Country' 4–6–2 No. 34006 *Bude*, having regained its feet after slipping on the greasy rail by the water crane, makes an impressive sight as it approaches the level crossing at the eastern end of the station.

Heading an inter-regional train of Southern stock, 'King Arthur' class 4–6–0 No. 30777 *Sir Lamiel* takes advantage of the initial down grade to the east of Brockenhurst to regain speed after the station stop. The N15 was rostered for the 11.50 a.m. Bournemouth Central–Birmingham (Snow Hill) on 23.7.60, and might have taken the train as far as Oxford before handing over to a Western Region engine. *Sir Lamiel* has been preserved as part of the National Collection.

With conductor rail in position, Standard class 4 2–6–0 No. 76011 gives tongue with a six-coach stopping service from Bournemouth on leaving Brockenhurst on 6.2.67. The second carriage is a Standard Mark I that has been recently repainted in the new blue and grey livery, contrasting oddly with the traditional green of the rest of the train.

Leaning impressively into the banked curve west of Lyndhurst Road station, Standard 4 2–6–4T No. 80151 opens up after a signal check with a special train on 9.4.67. The preparation of this engine reflected great credit on those concerned, for it was a magnificent sight with its white-painted buffers and gleaming paintwork. Fortunately, 80151 was saved from scrap and is undergoing restoration to full working order, being one of the last locomotives to be built at Brighton Works.

In the autumn sunshine, class M7 0–4–4T No. 30328 puffs sedately across Setley Plain towards the junction with the 5.30 p.m. Lymington Pier–Brockenhurst service on 26.9.59. The two-coach push-pull set, numbered 385, was created in 1949 by the conversion of a pair of ex-LSWR 'Ironclad' corridor brake composites for auto-train work; when photographed they were still painted in the all-red livery adopted for secondary and branch line stock soon after Nationalization. Five such sets (381–5) were created for use on Western Section routes only.

The Lymington branch was one of the last outposts of steam on the south coast. On 6.2.67 the train consisted of two Bulleid coaches and a Standard 4 2–6–4T, drifting gently across the open wastes of Setley Plain with a Lymington Pier–Brockenhurst service. Under the grime it was just possible to decipher the number, 80146, but the remarkable thing was not another living creature in sight. How different it might be, twenty-five years later!

On a fine spring evening in April 1963 the old Drummond M7 0–4–4T No. 30379 and its two-coach push-pull set 611 start out from Lymington Town station on yet another journey to Brockenhurst. The Town had been opened in 1860, but it took another twenty-four years to extend the branch an extra $1/_2$ mile to the pier. The Lymington branch proved to be one of the last to feature steam. Having been electrified in 1967, it remains open as a 'basic railway'.

By the end of 1963 the few remaining Drummond M7 0–4–4Ts were becoming work-weary and increasingly decrepit. One Sunday morning in November No. 30480 had an additional Maunsell open carriage attached to the usual two-coach push-pull set, which caused the Edwardian engine to plod very slowly up the hill past Shirley Holmes on its way from Lymington Pier to Brockenhurst.

With the end of push-pull operation by the spring of 1964, branch engines were required to run round the train both at Brockenhurst and at Lymington. On 18.4.65 'Mickey Mouse' class 2 2–6–2T No. 41312 was the branch engine, blasting out of Lymington Pier over the level crossing leading to the Yarmouth ferry. The early Southern Railway lower quadrant signals with metal arms are worthy of note; there was a similar combination at the south end of Lymington Town station, too.

Being a branch line with steam traction made the Lymington route something of a *cause célèbre* in the mid-sixties. Several specials were run during the period immediately before electrification, with tank engines at either end to save problems running round such long trains. On 9.4.67 class 2 2–6–2T No. 41320 led the nine-coach rake on the return trip from Lymington Pier, making an all-out effort as the train wound through part of the New Forest west of Ampress Halt; Standard 4 2–6–4T No. 80151 brought up the rear.

Symbolic of many Southern branches, an M7 tank coupled to a push-pull train was the staple diet of the Lymington line from the 1930s until 1964. With the driving trailer stopped beneath the neat overall roof and the fireman having taken the opportunity to stoke up, 0–4–4T No. 30379 awaited the 'right away' before propelling its two-coach load across the river from Lymington Town to the Pier terminus one evening in April 1963.

Totton and the Fawley branch

With an unfamiliar locomotive in garter blue at the front of a special train, the signalman at Totton box leaned out of his window to get a closer look. Preserved class A4 4–6–2 *Sir Nigel Gresley* had regained its original LNER number 4498 (BR No. 60007) and was heading for Weymouth on 4.6.67. The buffet car was in the new blue and grey livery, while warning lights (for the level crossing) and conductor rails *in situ* indicated that electrification was only five weeks away.

Trains Cross Here – but not very often! Only two passenger services on weekdays were provided from Southampton to Fawley (there were three in the reverse direction, Mondays to Fridays only) so not many pictures of them seem to exist. On 2.4.60 the 4.06 p.m. from Southampton Central gave plenty of advance warning before approaching the ungated crossing at Trotts Lane near Marchwood, with class 2 2–6–2T No. 41293 in charge of three Standard Mark I corridors still painted in 'Blood and Custard' colours.

Even in the fifties and sixties, the Fawley branch relied on freight traffic to justify its existence. The 1.20 p.m. from Fawley conveyed unfitted oil tanker wagons for Spondon, requiring a couple of fitted 'runner' wagons to help engine braking and provide a buffer between the spark-throwing steam engines and their inflammable load. On 9.6.61 the train was double-headed by class H16 4–6–2T No. 30516 and Standard class 3 2–6–2T 82015 as it rumbled slowly over the ungated crossing at Pooksgreen, north of Marchwood; the tanks would hand over to a powerful tender engine (maybe an 8F 2–8–0 or 9F 2–10–0) at Bevois Park sidings or at Eastleigh.

A moment of history: a trial run was laid on for Sunday, 6.3.60, to see whether the Urie Pacific tanks could be used on Fawley oil trains successfully. Class H16 4–6–2T No. 30516 coped manfully with the 43-wagon test train loaded with coal – around 750 tons gross – and thundered through Marchwood on the outward run. As a result, the 96 ton H16 tanks visited Fawley regularly, and Marchwood gained a loop line to allow trains to pass on the single track route from Totton.

With the single line tablet released for the block section from Marchwood to Totton, the double-headed freight made ready to depart on St Patrick's Day, 1962. The oil-tank train from Fawley was powered by three-cylinder class W 2–6–4T No. 31922 and 'Mickey Mouse' class 2 2–6–2T No. 41311, a combination that would be replaced by a single large tender engine in the Southampton area or at Eastleigh in readiness for the next stage of the journey north.

Interest in the Southern's very American class USA 0–6–0T locomotives increased when a couple of those still based at Southampton Docks were painted in green. Both Nos 30064 and 30073 were selected for haulage of a special from London over the Fawley branch on 20.3.66. With 30073 leading, the train attracted a great deal of lineside attention, not least in the wooded terrain between Marchwood and Hythe, bound for Fawley.

From the mid-sixties a new road was constructed to cater for the many petroleum tankers loading at Fawley Refinery, avoiding the villages of Marchwood and Hythe. At one location south-east of Hounsdown the single track railway crossed the new road on an impressive skew bridge: on 20.3.66 the pair of USA 0–6–0Ts pounded along the embankment with the RCTS special on the way back to Southampton with No. 30064 leading 30073, their smart green livery blending well both with the surroundings and the carriages of the train.

After an RCTS special over the Fawley branch proved so popular in 1966, the LCGB organized a similar visit the following year. Again, a brace of USA 0–6–0Ts was requested, the combination on this occasion consisting of Nos 30069 (in black livery) and 30064. The latter was the leading engine on the return trip on 9.4.67, the pair shuffling through a leafy cutting on the outskirts of Hythe before diving beneath one of the few overline bridges on this rural route.

Southampton and the surrounding area

For years Redbridge Sleeper Depot had been shunted by the little Drummond C14 0–4–0T 77s, then on its demise an 02 0–4–4T had fulfilled the role. Finally, one of the USA 0–6–0T engines from Southampton Docks was renumbered into departmental stock and became resident shunter. On 21.4.66 DS 233 (formerly No. 30061) sizzles outside its little stone shed close to the main line – of the fourteen USA tanks acquired after the war, this was the only one to have been built by Porter; its WD number was 1264.

First of the 'Merchant Navy' 4–6–2s to have been rebuilt in 1956, No. 35018 *British India Line* howls through Redbridge with the 'Down' 'Bournemouth Belle' Pullman on 31.1.59, passing an 'Up' train containing Maunsell stock. The sleeper depot is on the right. *British India Line* was saved from the scrap-yard and is now being restored at Ropley on the Mid-Hants Steam Railway.

On 30.4.61 the 'Solent Limited' special train visited the Meon Valley and Southampton Docks. Class USA 0–6–0T No. 30073 took the train on a complete circuit of the docks, entering at Millbrook and emerging at Canute Road. Amid a steady drizzle, 30073 crosses Herbert Walker Avenue in the New (Western) Docks towards 102 berth, used by Union Castle vessels. In the background, on the right, stands Rank's Solent Flour Mill.

A transfer freight from the New Docks to the Old Docks at Southampton needed to run the gauntlet of road traffic at the Town Quay. On 13.4.57 class E1 0–6–0T No. 32689 has a good head of steam as it shuffles across the junction at the lower end of High Street with a load of vans. In the background can be seen the Queen Mary baggage house, Seaway House and the remains of the old Watergate. This E1 tank engine was one of three to be fitted with radio equipment in 1955 for more efficient use around the docks – it was mounted on the cab roof. The 1883-built 32689 was withdrawn in 1960.

Passing the Royal Pier around midday on 12.3.60, class E2 0–6–0T No. 32101 trundles a van train from the New Docks by the roadside towards the Old Docks. Although allocated to 71A (Eastleigh) according to the shed plate, members of the ten-strong E2 class were drafted into Southampton Docks to replace withdrawn E1 locomotives on trip working and shunting duties. The railway link between Western and Eastern Docks was severed in 1979 and the track lifted at this point.

Built in 1893 at Nine Elms Works as No. 96 for the LSWR, then named *Normandy* for use in Southampton Docks, Adams class B4 0–4–0T No. 30096 had reached the ripe old age of sixty-eight years when it was found working once more in its former haunts, the Eastern (Old) Docks, on 9.6.61. The flat 90° crossing in the foreground is of interest, as well as the typical industrial building behind the engine. *Normandy* has been restored to LSWR condition and active use on the Bluebell Railway in Sussex.

It was rather unusual for passenger trains (e.g. boat trains) to run between the New Docks and Old Docks since each had direct connection to the main line at Millbrook or Southampton Terminus respectively. During the special LCGB tour of 30.4.61 USA 0–6–0T No. 30073 carried out a complete circuit of the docks, seen here beside Platform Road with the Town Quay in the left background. Note the loop line and loading gauge.

In the Empress Dock (Eastern Docks) Fyffes' bananas were a major source of traffic for many years. On 7.2.66 old and new forms of railway shunting engine could be seen side by side: Ruston & Hornsby diesel-electric 0–6–0D D2988 stood with USA 0–6–0T No. 30069 outside the sheds at 24/25 berths, exhibiting duty discs Ex 1 and Ex 2 respectively.

A train-load of fitted banana vans is eased out of the Empress yard in the Eastern Docks by one of the competent and reliable Urie class S15 4–6–0s, No. 30509. On the right an E2 0–6–0T is engaged in shunting, while on the left more wagons await attention. The amount of rail-borne traffic in the Old Docks alone was still considerable, and the working timetable recorded a steady stream of departures from mid-morning onwards. No. 30509 headed the 11.55 a.m for Salisbury on 9.6.61.

Summer Saturdays at Southampton Central could be very entertaining, with a procession of trains in all directions for much of the day. On 3.8.57 the first of the Lymington boat trains – the 9.42 a.m. from Waterloo to Lymington Pier – was headed by a 'Schools' 4–4–0, which would take the express as far as Brockenhurst before handing over to a smaller engine for the last part of the journey. With distinctive three-disc headcode, class V No. 30907 *Dulwich*, gleaming in brunswick green paint-work, pulls smartly away from platform 4 under clear signals with an ex-GWR corridor in 'Blood and Custard' colours next to the tender.

In the final few months of steam, even express locomotives were to be found on humdrum duties far below their status. On 6.2.67 Bulleid 'Merchant Navy' 4–6–2 No. 35014 *Nederland Line* shuffles past Hampshire diesel unit 1109 with a handful of vans bound for the Western Docks; amazingly, the name-plate was still *in situ* at this late stage. The location is midway between Southampton Central station and Millbrook.

Sixty years old, but in sparkling form, class T9 'Greyhound' 4–4–0 No. 30120 was selected for an enthusiasts' special to Swindon on 3.1.60. Looking very smart, the superheated Drummond engine was all ready to go at Southampton Central by 10.30 a.m., carrying class 'A' headlamps in place of the usual discs as it was to venture onto the Western Region at Reading. On a damp, murky morning the special train stood in platform 1 with the clock tower behind – a very different style of architecture from today's Southampton station.

One of the more unusual workings on a summer Saturday during the peak season was the 9.27 a.m. Wimbledon–Weymouth. With an assortment of stock, class S15 4–6–0 No. 30828 strode away from the Southampton Central stop – Brockenhurst the next station. The Bulleid brake composite carriage immediately behind the engine was still in the experimental 'Plum and Spilt Milk' colour scheme once associated with the LNWR but tested by British Railways in the early days of Nationalization; the date was 3.8.57. Saved from scrap, this Maunsell engine has been reconditioned at Eastleigh Works and soon will be running once again, restored to 1930s Southern Railway livery.

With the station in the middle of rebuilding and conductor rails in position alongside the running lines, an original Bulleid 'Spam Can' of the 'West Country' class sets out from Southampton Central with a Bournemouth–Waterloo express on 27.10.66. No. 34006 *Bude* has its electric headlights on as it gathers way towards the tunnel, passing the site of the nineteenth-century Blechynden station.

Rebuilt 'West Country' 4–6–2 No. 34039 *Boscastle* steams out of the tunnel from Southampton Central towards Northam junction with an 'Up' express from Weymouth to Waterloo on 23.7.60. In this area, known as St Mary's, rows of terraced houses backed onto the railway cutting before the road system was completely changed. Now the former 'Up' and 'Down' main lines have been re-signalled to allow for bi-directional running through the tunnel, while the triangle of tracks at Northam (which allowed through running into Southampton Terminus station or the Old Docks) is no more.

In the lee of the Ocean Terminal building, beside berths 43 and 44 in the Eastern Docks, class B4 0–4–0T No. 30096 simmers patiently with three Standard Mark I carriages while rain comes in gusts from the south-west. It was waiting to depart for Winchester (Chesil) with a LCGB special on 9.3.63. The tour was repeated some weeks later when the appalling weather conditions abated. Since restoration on the Bluebell Railway, this engine has again had a spell of passenger train haulage when it was loaned to the Swanage line for a season.

On Sunday, 26.6.60, a boat train for London (Waterloo) crosses Canute Road at the regulation walking pace in the care of 'Schools' class 4–4–0 No. 30912 *Downside*. Dock Gate 3 was the normal exit for trains from the Eastern Docks. It was more usual to have the train 'flagged' across Canute Road, but on this occasion a policeman was on duty; road users seem to be restricted to a few cyclists. The notice about cross-Channel and Channel Island steamers (left) is of historic interest now.

Standard 4 2–6–0 No. 76028 drifts slowly across Canute Road past Southampton Terminus station with a mixed freight for the docks on 12.3.60 under the watchful eye of the flagman. The first few wagons have refrigerated containers, while beyond is the huge goods depot erected in 1880. Today a single track across Canute Road is rusty and disused, while the Terminus station has been closed since 1966. A new container port for freightliner trains has been constructed at Millbrook.

Making a rare foray onto the main line, Adams class B4 0–4–0T No. 30096 bustles past the large goods depot, seen from the platforms of Southampton Terminus station, on 9.3.63. It headed a special from the Ocean Terminal platform in the Old Docks to Winchester (Chesil), the former DN&SR station closed from March 1960 to passenger traffic. The seventy-year-old former dock tank *Normandy* was sold off for further service to Corralls at the end of 1963 and is now preserved.

In the midst of a heavy downpour on 15.7.61, the 4.50 p.m from Southampton Terminus to Andover Junction was signalled away. On greasy rails a restrained departure was called for, and WR 'Mogul' No. 6327 duly obliged. Most passenger services to Andover were provided by the Hampshire diesel multiple units, but this was one of the last steam duties, stopping at all stations – probably a balancing working for the M&SWJ route, which closed to all traffic north of Ludgershall from 11.9.61.

On a hot summer Saturday, class S15 4–6–0 No. 30507 plodded steadily past Southampton Terminus station with a trainload of assorted wagons from the Eastern Docks. At the front were several Conflat containers while, beside the goods depot, serried ranks of vans waited to be loaded or unloaded for onward transmission in subsequent freight services. Beneath the station canopy a T9 'Greyhound' 4–4–0 was having the fire made up in preparation for a local train to Portsmouth; the date was 15.6.57.

Months after the last official steam had ceased on the Southern, some activity could still be found if one knew where to look for it. On a crisp March day in 1968, the *Corrall Queen* (alias B4 0–4–0T No. 30096) sets off across Britannia Road past the gasworks with some wagons for Dibles Wharf. Once there had been three 'tramways' connecting the main line at Northam with various Itchen quays and wharves, but this was the only one to remain in use by the late 1960s.

Over the Hamble River to Fareham

Bursledon before the 'bus stop' image; on 21.6.61 light engine No. 76014 gathers pace past the signal cabin heading for Southampton in the strong evening sun. Since the sixties the only recognizable landmark has been the foot-bridge, for the signal-box and traditional station buildings were demolished; in the eighties the platforms were tidied up and CLASP-type waiting shelters installed, with co-operation from Hampshire County Council.

The Netley line from Portswood (St Denys) was opened in 1866, but it took until 1889 to extend it eastward as far as Fareham. One of the major obstacles was constructing a bridge across the Hamble River at Bursledon: many locomotive classes were banned from the route altogether, while others were restricted with regard to speed or double-heading. A complete stranger that was permitted, in the final months of steam, was the Gresley K4 2–6–0 No. 3442 (formerly BR No. 61994) *The Great Marquess*, pictured negotiating the bridge on 12.3.67 with a special train from London (Victoria).

A favourite running-in turn for locomotives overhauled at Eastleigh Works (if they weren't too big or heavy) was the 9.07 a.m Fareham–Netley pick-up goods. On 2.4.60 Standard class 4 2–6–4T No. 80083 had the task, there being several empty oil tankers for Hamble Road Sidings in the train. The immaculate 80083 drew out of the goods yard at Swanwick, the buffers of the unfitted tank wagons banging and clanging until a rhythm was established. Swanwick was once an important centre for Hampshire strawberry traffic.

The elegant 'Brighton Atlantic' class H2 locomotives were quite regular performers on the 9.40 a.m. Brighton–Bournemouth West and 1.50 p.m. return service during the early 1950s. On 16.7.55 No. 32421 *South Foreland* was the engine, displaying the appropriate three-disc headcode by the original 1841-built part of Fareham station during a brief pause for water on the eastbound journey. Westbound, the train passed through Fareham non-stop between Chichester and Southampton at around 10.45 a.m.

Within four years of Nationalization, new BR Standard class 4 2–6–0s were being delivered to the Southern Region to replace superannuated 4–4–0s on local and semi-fast passenger trains. The first fifteen were numbered 76005–19 and allocated to Eastleigh, soon appearing on Portsmouth to Bristol or Cardiff inter-regional services. On 18.7.59 No. 76005 took over the Saturdays only 7.49 a.m. Bristol (Temple Meads)–Brighton at Salisbury; this was one of those summer Saturday trains that ran for a very limited period, in this instance for just five Saturdays in the season. This service was first operated on 18 July, and 76005 was pictured breasting the summit of the 1 in 91/81 to Swanwick while running non-stop between Southampton Central and Fareham with a ten-coach load.

On weekdays throughout the year there were three through trains from Brighton to destinations in the west (with an equivalent number of services in the opposite direction). The most prestigious was, without doubt, the Plymouth train since it boasted a restaurant car throughout; a Portsmouth portion was added (or subtracted) at Fareham. On 2.3.57 the combined Brighton and Portsmouth to Plymouth service featured 'West Country' 4–6–2 No. 34039 *Boscastle* in charge of the ten-coach train, getting to grips with the 1 in 100/112 upgrade out of Fareham beneath Gudge Heath Lane bridge.

By 1957 only one 'Atlantic' remained serviceable, so substitutes were tried out on the Brighton–Bournemouth duty. On 25.5.57 a former SECR class L 4–4–0 brings the 1.50 p.m. Bournemouth West–Brighton into Fareham's platform 2 past gantries of semaphore signals and period gas lighting. No. 31776 was one of a pair of Borsig-built locomotives based at 75A at the time, but they were not as popular as the surviving class H2 4–4–2, No. 32424 *Beachy Head*; in due course 'Schools' class 4–4–0s became available, so the problem was resolved.

In pouring rain, class M7 0–4–4T No. 30356 prepares to depart from platform 3 at Fareham with the 10.45 a.m. Portsmouth & Southsea–Eastleigh service (via Knowle Halt) on 9.2.57. In the background a four-wheeled PMV has been shunted alongside the cattle dock. The Hampshire diesel multiple unit programme was introduced progressively from June 1957, with complete implementation on local services by October of that year.

Following the Kent coast electrification in 1959, some locomotives migrated westwards to seek further employment. Eastleigh shed took on a solitary Maunsell rebuild of a SECR design, which had a turn alongside the handful of surviving Drummond 4–4–0s on local passenger and van trains. On 4.2.61 class D1 No. 31735 sidles out of the loop in front of Fareham East signal-box with the 10.37 a.m. Salisbury–Portsmouth & Southsea vans, a regular duty at this period for elderly 4–4–0s involving a reversal at Southampton Terminus.

Creating its own brand of hoar-frost in the crisp, early morning conditions, class 2 2–6–2T No. 41293 clears its tubes in readiness for some sharp undulations with the 9.07 a.m. pick-up goods to Netley as it curves past the Fareham Co-op laundry on 15.2.60. Though built to an LMS design by H.G. Ivatt, at least twenty of these lively little engines spent their entire working lives on the Southern Region, construction continuing under BR until 1952.

One of the final activities for a member of the 'King Arthur' class was the 11.47 a.m. goods from Salisbury (East Yard) to Chichester. On 23.2.62 the task fell to No. 30770 *Sir Prianius*, seen passing Fareham East box immediately after surrendering the single line tablet for the section from Knowle junction through Funtley tunnel. In the 1990s part of Fareham's 'Down' goods yard remains open for stone traffic (ARC) which travels via Salisbury.

New Year 1962 (1): Following overnight snow, 'Black Motor' 0–6–0 No. 30306 crunches its way along the loop line in front of Fareham West signal-box with the delayed 7.50 a.m. Eastleigh–Gosport goods on 1.1.62. This elderly Drummond locomotive, built by Dubs of Glasgow in 1897, was withdrawn in April 1962; the last examples were broken up in 1964.

New Year 1962 (2): Because of the sudden cold snap, a Brighton class K 2–6–0 was commandeered for the 11.45 a.m. Portsmouth Harbour portion of the through service to Cardiff on 1.1.62. Having brought the four-coach set (888) tender-first from the harbour, No. 32343 ran round the train at Fareham and drew it on to the Gosport branch to allow the main portion (the 11.00 a.m. from Brighton) to use the same platform. Then the Portsmouth coaches would be shunted back onto the rear of the main train ready for onward conveyance to Cardiff.

New Year 1962 (3): Drifting round the sharp curve into Fareham station, rebuilt 'West Country' 4–6–2 No. 34008 *Padstow* was in charge of the 11.00 a.m. Brighton–Cardiff through service on 1.1.62. The spotless brunswick green paintwork of the Bulleid locomotive contrasted with the more grubby green of the Southern carriages amid the snow, smoke and steam being whipped away by the keen northerly wind.

For a couple of Sundays in November 1964 a number of services over the Waterloo–Southampton section of the Bournemouth main line were diverted between Eastleigh and St Denys, running via Fareham. On the first occasion, on 22.11.64, the 'Down' 'Bournemouth Belle' had a change of engine at platform 2, departing 'wrong line' towards Netley with rebuilt 'West Country' 4–6–2 No. 34046 *Braunton* attached. The camera captured a moment when the big engine's wheels spun out of control on the greasy rails before the heavy Pullman train could make a more dignified exit from this unusual diversion.

On weekdays the 4.20 p.m. from Havant and the 5.35 p.m. from Gosport combined at Fareham to form the 6.29 p.m. goods for Eastleigh. On 23.6.61 class Q 0–6–0 No. 30532 was priming profusely as it struggled away from platform 3, signalled via the steeply-graded double-track route avoiding Funtley tunnel. The resultant 'clag' could be seen for miles!

Just as the days of local passenger trains with steam haulage were numbered, so time was running out for the antique ex-LSWR non-corridor carriages that had been such a familiar aspect of these services since Edwardian times. After a heavy shower of rain, 'Mickey Mouse' class 2 2–6–2T No. 41293 was taking water at Fareham in charge of the 11.18 a.m. Portsmouth & Southsea–Andover Junction train with one of the old South Western sets in tow – the route was via the Netley line to Southampton, calling at all stations. The date was 9.2.57. Note the lower-quadrant signals in the 'Up' goods yard.

After the everyday sight of Hampshire diesels on local trains since mid-1957, it was unexpected to find the 3.07 p.m. Portsmouth & Southsea–Reading General service provided by one of the new Pressed Steel three-car units on 19.5.61. This train had for years offered the opportunity to see a former GWR locomotive at Fareham but, in spite of modernization, the timetable still allowed five minutes wait there – to take water, perhaps?

Two locomotives that, individually, were no strangers to Fareham, were to be seen there in double-harness on 20.3.66. Surrounded by period trappings of the steam age – gas lighting, semaphore signals, platform barrow, water cranes – class U 2–6–0 No. 31639 and Standard 4 4–6–0 No. 75070 gave tongue in great style with a return special to London via Havant, pounding through platform 2 without hesitation.

Farewell to Fareham. The setting sun was prophetic, for 1962 was to mark the end of the through service between Brighton and Bournemouth. On 21.5.62 'Schools' 4–4–0 No. 30923 *Bradfield* whisked the 6.35 p.m. Bournemouth West–Brighton train away from Fareham past the Advanced Starter signal, this class of engine being ideal for an undulating route with few stops and a load that never exceeded 300 tons gross.

The Gosport line

After the success of a special excursion to Gosport during February 1966, a repeat visit was organized by the RCTS for 20.3.66. As the triangle was no longer available for turning engines at Gosport, class U 2–6–0 No. 31639 was obliged to run tender-first on the return leg, in which mode it was recorded passing through the intermediate station of Fort Brockhurst on the single line. A 'skew' level crossing justified retention of the Home signal there.

The original LSWR branch, from Bishopstoke to Gosport (for Portsmouth), opened in November 1841 and lost its passenger traffic in June 1953, but freight and parcels continued to flourish. On 25.9.61 the 7.50 a.m. goods from Eastleigh, after a spell of shunting, made a vigorous start from Fareham towards Gosport behind class U 2–6–0 No. 31613. Having been double track, the line was singled south of Fareham as an economy measure in the thirties.

From Redlands Lane there was an excellent view of the regular morning goods as it plodded away from Fareham towards Fort Brockhurst on the embankment. Class Q 0–6–0 No. 30536 was the engine in charge on 26.3.60, while the train was the usual mixture of freight wagons and parcels van for Gosport. The line remained open throughout until 1969, after which it was cut back to Bedenham.

80

With the regulator almost closed, class 4 2–6–0 No. 76012 was able to manage the final stage of the 1 in 466 gradient up from Fort Brockhurst towards Fareham without difficulty on 4.2.61. The train was the 2.15 p.m. from Gosport which, after shunting the interchange sidings at Bedenham on the outward journey, returned non-stop to Fareham. The wide embankment was a reminder of the days when this route was double track.

In the final years of steam operation of freight traffic over the Gosport line, BR Standard designs took over. Class 4 engines, both 2–6–0 tender and 2–6–4T, became the mainstay although the tanks were preferred to avoid tender-first running. The regime is typified by this study of 2–6–4T No. 80066 at Fort Brockhurst with the 5.35 p.m. goods and parcels service from Gosport to Fareham in June 1963. Note that the track through the 'Down' platform has been lifted.

There was a galaxy of gricers at Gosport to greet the first special passenger train to reach there since services were suspended in June 1953. The occasion was the centenary of the Portsmouth Direct line, opened in 1859, but the star was undoubtedly 1897-built class 700 0–6–0 No. 30350. It arrived from Fareham tender-first, then turned on the Stokes Bay triangle in readiness for the long haul back from Fareham to London chimney-first via Havant. The ruins of Sir William Tite's magnificent terminus, constructed in 1841 but bombed one hundred years later, can be seen on the right; the date was 25.1.59.

Panoramic view of Gosport: by a foot-bridge close to where the former engine shed was situated, class N 2–6–0 No. 31411 poses for a moment in the winter sunshine for the benefit of photographers while running round a special train on 20.2.66. The 'Mogul' was one of the final series of Woolwich Arsenal kits purchased by the Southern; by this time it was based at Guildford (70C).

With both sets of level crossing gates open at Spring Garden Lane and Mumby Road, class N 2–6–0 No. 31413 reverses through Gosport station to pick up some wagons from RN Clarence Yard beyond on 9.5.62. On weekdays the goods arrived at Gosport at around midday, which left ample time to visit the Victualling Yard if necessary as departure was not scheduled until 2.15 p.m. Working Timetable instructions for this train were: 'Set down can of water at Cambridge Road crossing'.

Knowle and the Meon Valley

Usually the preserve of a husky 4–6–0, on 27.5.61 the 11.47 a.m. Salisbury–Chichester goods was entrusted to Standard class 4 2–6–0 No. 76013. With the safety valves just blowing off, the 'Mogul' rumbled out of Funtley tunnel all ready to increase speed as soon as it rounded the sharp curve at the south end of Fareham station. A true mixed-traffic design, the Southern made very good use of its various Standard classes.

A rare chance to record the seldom-noticed activities of the weed-killing train on Southern metals occurred on 24.5.61. Consisting of a couple of adapted long-wheelbase vans of Maunsell design plus several chemical tank wagons, the train was being propelled along the single track north of Funtley tunnel towards Knowle by Standard class 4 2–6–0 No. 76053; this location was the disused brickworks' siding close to the abattoir. Note the extension arms (which would have been retracted while negotiating stations or tunnels), the electrification warning flash and the headcode disc.

One of the hazards of calling at Knowle Halt! Three-car Hampshire diesel set 1114 formed the 12.42 p.m. Andover Junction–Portsmouth & Southsea calling at all stations on 23.12.60, but when a couple of passengers joined the train at Knowle's short platform the guard was unable to reach them to issue or check tickets as the brake compartment was at the wrong end of the set. . . . When constructed, in 1957, unit 1114 had comprised only two coaches, but was enlarged later.

Looking well burnished in the winter sun, 4900 class 4–6–0 No. 5969 *Honington Hall* gives a spirited performance while ascending the 1 in 100 gradient from Fareham towards Knowle junction on 25.2.61. The 81D-based engine is coupled to a Bulleid three-coach set forming the 3.07 p.m. Portsmouth & Southsea–Reading General service, a common enough combination on weekdays throughout the year until replaced by a WR DMU three months later.

With the last rays of sun glinting off the tapered boiler, 4–6–0 No. 5927 *Guild Hall* battles toward the summit of the 1 in 100 up from Fareham on the Funtley deviation route with a return excursion to Cleethorpes on 25.6.61. This unusual working was pictured in the cutting above Highlands Road bridge, the ER Gresley stock being seldom seen in the Portsmouth area.

With a hint of spring in the air, freshly-overhauled Standard class 4 2–6–4T No. 80065 – based at Tonbridge in Kent (73J) – begins to weave across the tracks at Knowle junction with an afternoon goods to Eastleigh on 23.2.62. The train has come up from Fareham through Funtley tunnel and past Knowle Halt on the single line, to rejoin the double track deviation route at the junction before continuing to Eastleigh: the Meon Valley branch bears away towards Wickham at this point (far left of picture).

The weekday 9.10 a.m. Reading General–Portsmouth & Southsea was regularly worked by a WR engine (frequently a 'Hall' 4–6–0) throughout the year. But on 23.4.60 a double-chimney 'Schools' 4–4–0 was in charge, possibly borrowed to cover a last-minute failure. Class V No. 30918 *Hurstpierpoint* shot through the short, straight bore of Tapnage tunnel with Bulleid set 791 in tow before easing for the junction ahead, as the train was booked to call at Knowle Halt on the single track route to Fareham.

In a fine drizzle the 2.15 p.m. Droxford–Fareham goods shuffles past Knowle junction signal-box on 23.12.60, about to exchange the single line tablet for the Meon Valley branch with the token for the section through Funtley tunnel. The use of two brake vans can be seen clearly in this view from the signal-box, a practice that began with the freight-only period in February 1955. The engine on this occasion was class U 2–6–0 No. 31615.

Christmas Eve freight at Wickham: the 12.20 p.m. from Fareham to Droxford was allowed up to three-quarters of an hour for shunting the yard here. On 24.12.59 it had just arrived behind Standard class 4 2–6–0 No. 76028, sporting a good head of steam, a string of open wagons sandwiched between the usual two brake vans. The passing loop and 'Down' platform had been taken out of use not long after withdrawal of passenger traffic in 1955, signalling and the intermediate block post being dispensed with also, but the station and 'Up' platform remained remarkably tidy.

Not many special passenger trains traversed the southern stump of the Meon Valley line after services were suspended in February 1955, but one of the most interesting was sighted on 30.4.61. Two Victorian tank engines took over the excursion at Fareham to visit Droxford and Gosport in turn. The special is seen leaving Wickham for Droxford with class E1 0–6–0T No. 32694 leading and 02 0–4–4T No. 30200 next to the Mark 1 brake; the trailing point led into the goods yard.

From the vantage point of the rear brake van, this picture records the Home signal at the approach to Droxford from the south on 14.4.55, before simplification of the track layout, despite withdrawal of passenger services over the entire Meon Valley line in February 1955. Freight traffic between Fareham and Droxford continued until April 1962, and the long headshunt on the left was not lifted – it was there that the wartime Allies had held a secret conference on board a train before D-Day in 1944.

The Meon Valley goods was normally allocated to a tender locomotive, but on 21.3.62 the opportunity was taken to run-in Standard class 4 2–6–4T No. 80151 after overhaul at Eastleigh Works. Leaving a couple of wagons and the second brake van in the platform, the big tank engine and first brake van drew forward to shunt Wickham goods yard. Freight facilities were to be withdrawn after 27.4.62, so this may have been the only occasion the type visited this rural line.

Droxford for Hambledon: so stated the station nameboard, six years after closure. Class E1 0–6–0T No. 32694 and 02 0–4–4T No. 30200 brought the 'Solent Limited' excursion from Fareham up the Meon Valley line on 30.4.61, basking in the attention of photographers before running round to take the special back and on to Gosport.

Before closure in February 1955, the passenger service over the Meon Valley branch was provided by a push-pull train for much of the day. Something of that former atmosphere was recalled during the visit of a special on 7.3.59, consisting of motor train set No. 6 and Drummond M7 0–4–4T No. 30111. Droxford station still exists, and is now adapted as a fine country residence complete with canopy.

After closure, the Knowle junction–Wickham–Droxford section of the Meon Valley line was leased to Sadler-Vectrail, primarily for the development and testing of a lightweight diesel railcar. For comparative purposes, one of the ancient Stroudley 'Terrier' class A1x 0–6–0T locomotives made redundant by closure of the Hayling Island railway was acquired together with a Bulleid carriage. No. 32646 was at rest between the platforms at Droxford station on 7.11.65, but is now active again in the Isle of Wight after a spell as the 'Hayling Billy' pub sign.

North of Droxford, as far as Farringdon, the Meon Valley line closed completely upon withdrawal of passenger services in February 1955. Scenes like this, recalling leisurely summer days when the pick-up goods called at Privett hauled by a Drummond 'Bulldog' 4–4–0, belong to a vanished age: class L12 No. 30420 received the early style of BR livery, unlined black, in 1948, and this charming view was most likely recorded during the summer of 1949 or 1950. Most of the class, including 30420, went for scrap in 1951; the last survivor (No. 30434) was withdrawn when the Meon Valley line closed.

E.C. Griffith

Though officially closed from April 1962, the southern rump of the Meon Valley branch did see further use. On 5.6.62 a trainload of redundant wooden-bodied open wagons was dispersed among the sidings at Droxford to await breaking-up, where class Q 0–6–0 No. 30543 was noted during the shunting operations. Later, the engine returned to Fareham with the pair of brake vans. It had acquired a single chimney of BR Standard pattern around this time, in place of the Bulleid fashion with double blastpipe.

Botley, Bishop's Waltham, Swaythling and Eastleigh

The Branch Lines Society's special train bustles away from Botley on 7.3.59 bound for Fareham, Droxford and Gosport after its visit to Bishop's Waltham. Immaculate class M7 0–4–4T No. 30111 powered the two-coach push-pull set (No. 6), which consisted of a former SECR compartment carriage and an ex-LSWR driving trailer. As No. 111 the locomotive had been built for the LSWR in 1904 and was scrapped in 1964; push-pull control gear was fitted in 1930.

Botley station was host to a push-pull train on 7.3.59, not an operation that was normally associated with the Fareham–Eastleigh line. Class M7 0–4–4T No. 30111 and its motor train had just travelled over the long-closed Bishop's Waltham branch for the benefit of enthusiasts, prior to a visit to the Meon Valley and Gosport lines. Botley had opened in November 1841 as an intermediate station on the Gosport branch; the fine building on the 'Up' platform was demolished many years ago and replaced by a simple shelter.

A highly unusual sight on the Southampton main line, USA class 0–6–0T No. 30073 plods through Swaythling station with the 'Solent Limited' special, having completed a tour of both New and Old Docks, on its way to Eastleigh on 30.4.61. At this period the 'Down' Home signal here was still a lower-quadrant example, just visible beyond the canopy.

Against the splendid architecture of Bishop's Waltham station, which opened in June 1863, the branch goods train brews up in readiness for the return to Botley on St David's Day, 1962. Designed for the LMS in 1946, the Ivatt class 2 2–6–2T was an attractive and useful little engine. No. 41214 had but recently been transferred to the Southern and, following closure of the Bishop's Waltham branch to all traffic after 27.4.62, migrated further west to Barnstaple (for the Torrington–Halwill line).

A sight for sore eyes! Motorists travelling along the B3035 road between Bishop's Waltham and Curdridge on 7.3.59 must have been amazed to see a real live passenger train trundling along the freight-only branch line from Botley. By culvert 5A, road and rail were no more than a few yards apart, scarcely a mile south west of Bishop's Waltham, which lost its passenger service in January 1933. The BLS special consisted of Drummond M7 tank No. 30111 and push-pull set No. 6, seen here returning towards Botley.

Once intended as an intermediate station on a cross-country route to Petersfield, Bishop's Waltham never progressed beyond a pleasant country terminus. Losing its passenger traffic in 1933, it remained open for freight for a further twenty-nine years. Five weeks before total closure, class 2 2–6–2T No. 41293 was about to leave Bishop's Waltham with a single coal wagon and brake van forming the 11.10 a.m. goods to Botley on 21.3.62. J.E. Smith's coal lorry was obtaining fresh supplies from the truck alongside, delivered by the 10 a.m. train that morning.

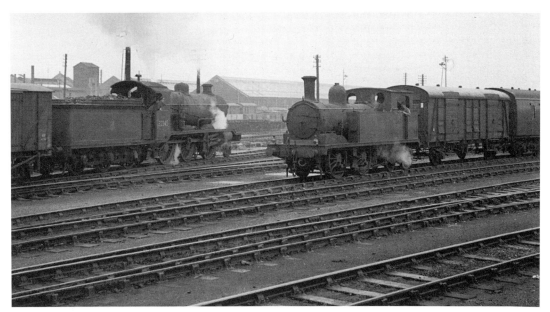

Even as late as 1961 the view from Eastleigh's platform 4 was very traditional – against the background of the wagon and carriage works at Barton Park, class K 2–6–0 No. 32345 set out with the 10.03 a.m. goods for Fratton Yard, while Adams 02 0–4–4T No. 30223 indulged in some carriage piloting. The date was 29.5.61.

With safety valves lifting, Standard class 4 2–6–0 No. 76025 approaches Campbell Road bridge with a train of loaded oil tanks on 7.8.57. The oil tankers would have come from Fawley, with an engine change at Bevois Park sidings. Access to Eastleigh MPD was by way of the tracks to the left of the main line, the shed itself being hidden by the trees. The so-called 'Dorset siding' was on the right.

The Edwardian era survived, in transport terms, until the fifties: beneath the ornate foot-bridge linking Eastleigh's two island platforms a complete ex-LSWR train stands at platform 2. Oozing steam from all manner of places, push-pull set No. 1 and M7 0–4–4T No. 30125 (at the rear) prepare to keep passengers warm aboard the 3.59 p.m. service to Alton on 18.2.56. Mid-Hants trains were modernized in late 1957 when diesel multiple units began to serve Itchen Abbas, Alresford, Ropley, Medstead & Four Marks and Alton at regular intervals.

By the mid-sixties it seemed as if the world and his wife came out every time there was some special train to see. Leaving Eastleigh on 29.8.65 bound for Weymouth, 'West Country' 4–6–2 No. 34019 *Bideford* drew the crowds to its excitable three-cylinder beat as it approached Campbell Road bridge with a rather mixed rake of Standard carriages.

Shawford junction, Winchester and beyond

In full cry, a 'Merchant Navy' steamed northwards towards Shawford junction with a Weymouth–Waterloo express on 18.9.60. No. 35027 *Port Line* was the engine, one of ten constructed after Nationalization but rebuilt in 1957. Sent for scrap in 1966, this machine has been meticulously restored to working order over many years.

On Saturdays during the summer peak there was a constant procession of trains passing Shawford junction in either direction. Important through services to the WR carried reporting numbers, identifying them to signalmen where the use of class 'A' headlamps alone might not be enough. On 21.6.58 4–6–0 No. 7911 *Lady Margaret Hall* displayed reporting number 978 as it thundered towards Shawford station with the 1.11 p.m. Portsmouth Harbour–Birmingham (Moor Street) express.

The dulcet exhaust note of a four-cylinder 'Lord Nelson' 4–6–0 was still quite commonplace on the Waterloo–Southampton–Bournemouth main line in 1960, so the appearance of No. 30858 *Lord Duncan* at the head of an 'Up' boat train from Southampton Docks on 5.3.60 excited no special interest at the time. Well-groomed and in fine fettle, 30858 was passing Shawford junction in the direction of Winchester (City); tracks linking Winchester (Chesil) with the main line can be seen curving away on the left.

After being checked at the signal, Standard class 4 4–6–0 No. 75005 was opened up as it set off across the points at Shawford junction with the 12.08 p.m. Eastleigh–Newbury service on the final day of passenger traffic over the southern part of the former Didcot, Newbury & Southampton Railway (between Winchester Chesil and Newbury) on 5.3.60.

In the deep cutting south of Winchester City station, 'Battle of Britain' 4–6–2 No. 34066 *Spitfire* accelerates a boat train for Southampton Docks via Millbrook onward on 27.8.66. *Spitfire* was the unfortunate engine to have been involved in the Lewisham disaster during fog, but after major repairs it was never rebuilt and was withdrawn for scrap not long after this picture was taken.

Streaking through the cutting approaching Winchester City station, rebuilt 'Battle of Britain' 4–6–2 No. 34077 *603 Squadron* was in charge of the 'Up' 'Bournemouth Belle' Pullman train for its non-stop run between Southampton Central and Waterloo on 27.8.66. This was one of the last summer Saturdays on which observers could relish the sight and sound of the steam-hauled 'Belle', for electrification spelled the end of this prestige service. In its final months a Type 4 Brush diesel (class 47) locomotive was normally provided.

On a bright autumn morning the Winchester City shunter pauses by the water column between spells of activity. Class B4 0–4–0T No. 30096 worked turn and turn about with No. 30102, there being a small locomotive depot for one engine in the yard on the 'Up' side. It was the sharpness of the curves in this yard that justified retention of such elderly machines, both of which were constructed in 1893. The date was 29.10.62.

Although passenger services were withdrawn from the DN&S route in March 1960, it remained open for through freight traffic and very occasional excursions. One of the latter travelled over the line on 25.6.61, when 'Mogul' No. 6367 swept round the curve from the Hockley viaduct to Shawford junction with Gresley stock from Cleethorpes – excursion duty 1X38. The 31-arch viaduct is a 'listed' structure and remains in place more than a quarter of a century after the last train ran over it.

Just a month before closure, the 2.12 p.m. Eastleigh–Newbury train gallops along the embankment beside the Winchester bypass, shortly after leaving the Hockley viaduct. One of the later 'Moguls', No. 7327 is travelling over the 1891 link with the former LSWR main line at Shawford junction, bound for Winchester Chesil station on 6.2.60.

Regular motive power over the DN&S line was the Collett 2251 class. One week before passenger services were withdrawn, 0–6–0 No. 2240 restarts the 9.08 a.m. Newbury–Eastleigh train from Winchester Chesil passing the brick-built signal cabin in the shadow of St Giles' hill. A characteristic GWR foot-bridge can be glimpsed in the background, with the end-loading dock on the left; a car-park occupies the site today.

The DN&S line was no stranger to four-coupled passenger engines, having been host to GWR 'Duke' class locomotives between the wars, while ex-LSWR 'Greyhounds' had a regular duty in the late fifties. But a most unusual visitor brought the 'North Hampshire Downsman' excursion to the route on 22.5.60; ex-SECR class E1 4–4–0 No. 31067 plodded slowly up the daunting 1 in 106 from Sutton Scotney on the single line towards Winchester Chesil with its eight-coach load, returning the same way later in the day.

Not far from the site of its derailment at Whitchurch (Town) in September 1954, Standard class 4 2–6–0 No. 76017 was heading south with the 9.50 a.m. Didcot–Eastleigh goods on 6.2.60 between Whitchurch and Sutton Scotney. As the winter sun slowly cleared the freezing fog, the engine's exhaust was highlighted against the cutting – note the use of a WR headlamp code rather than SR headcode discs. No. 76017 has been saved from scrap and is now in working order on the Mid-Hants line, based at Ropley.

Basingstoke, Andover and Salisbury area

In the last full summer of steam operations in the south, there were still some unusual Saturday activities to record. On 27.8.66 both 'Up' and 'Down' inter-regional services between Bournemouth and Newcastle were steam-hauled by Stanier class 5 4–6–0s. The 'Up' train passed Basingstoke 'C' signal-box with No. 45493 adorned with Southern-style headcode discs, a clean exhaust belying the explosive sounds as the regulator was opened for the run to Reading and beyond.

With many indications of impending electrification, rebuilt 'Merchant Navy' 4–6–2 No. 35014 *Nederland Line* clanks into Basingstoke station with the 11.10 a.m. Bournemouth–Waterloo express on Saturday, 27.8.66, the filthy external condition of the engine no doubt disguising its ability to perform what was required (and maybe, a little more). The MPD, 70D, was situated to the north of the running lines, behind the locomotive.

Standard class 5 4–6–0 No. 73018 had charge of the 11.15 a.m. Waterloo–Weymouth semi-fast on Saturday, 27.8.66. As the regulator was opened and steam released into the cylinders (and one or two other places not originally intended by Mr Riddles), the train began to ease forwards from Basingstoke's island platform in the direction of Worting junction. A WR DMU was in the adjoining platform, bound for Salisbury.

Beyond Worting junction the Salisbury route diverges from the Southampton line at Battledown summit: a flyover carries the 'Up' track from Southampton over the 'Up' and 'Down' Salisbury tracks. On 18.10.58 an 'Up' van train from Southampton, drawn by Urie S15 4–6–0 No. 30502, negotiates the flyover.

Topping the 1 in 194 gradient up from Hurstbourne, original 'Spam Can' 4–6–2 No. 34051 *Winston Churchill* of Salisbury shed made music with its three-cylinder beat, heading the 8.10 a.m. conditional freight working from Templecombe to Basingstoke on 27.2.60 at the approach to Whitchurch North station. This locomotive hauled the funeral train of its great namesake in 1965 and is now preserved as part of the National Collection.

On a bright winter morning Standard class 5 4–6–0 No. 73086 *The Green Knight* briskly accelerates the 9.30 a.m. Waterloo–Salisbury service away from Whitchurch North. The 1854-built station still has a small goods yard in operation, complete with semaphore signals; the date is 27.2.60.

A link between Hurstbourne (on the West of England main line) and Fullerton, between Andover and Romsey, opened in 1885 but never achieved more than local traffic status; passenger traffic was discontinued in 1931 and the connection between Hurstbourne and Longparish severed. Even the freight service succumbed in May 1956 – the single wagon and brake van forming the 11.45 a.m. Longparish–Fullerton is typical of this rural backwater in its final years. Class T9 4–4–0 No. 30730 was pictured with the branch freight at Fullerton.

Lens of Sutton

'Britannia' Standard class 7 4–6–2s were not often seen on the SR West of England main line. No. 70020 *Mercury* appeared at Andover Junction with an enthusiasts' special in March 1964, paying a visit to Ludgershall on the former M&SWJ branch before continuing westward. Beautifully polished, *Mercury* made an impressive departure from Andover Junction with a full head of steam.

The Ludgershall branch saw several special trains in the final period of steam traction, as even the largest Pacific classes were permitted. Following such a visit on 9.10.66, rebuilt 'Merchant Navy' No. 35023 (formerly named *Holland Afrika Line*) curves away from the island platform onto the 'Up' main line in anticipation of a lively run back to London with the SCTS 'Four Counties Special'.

While the rambling cross-country former M&SWJ route between Andover Junction and Cheltenham had closed from September 1961, the short section from Red Post junction to Ludgershall remained open for goods traffic, primarily for the military authorities. The ex-GWR Tidworth branch had been taken over by the War Department in 1955, so retention of the link with the main line at Andover was sensible. On 12.5.62 class U 2–6–0 No. 31613 was coupled to a lengthy freight for Andover Junction at the 'Up' platform at Ludgershall.

A Sunday morning local train from Salisbury to Andover and Basingstoke produced the ultimate WR diesel-hydraulic 'Hymek' locomotive D7100 in charge on 20.3.66. Steam enthusiasts may be amused to note that most – if not all – the steam heating was diverted outside the Bulleid brake composite! The train was pictured near Porton.

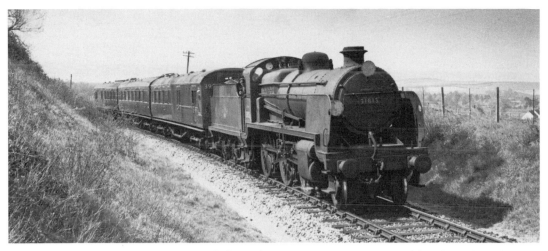

Services over the Bournemouth–Salisbury line were quite sparce, unlike the 'Old Road' to Brockenhurst. During the winter only five trains ran north on weekdays (four southbound) until late April when an additional one ran in each direction. On 30.4.60 class N 2–6–0 No. 31813 was rostered for the extra 'Up' service, the 10.04 a.m. Bournemouth West–Salisbury; with a Maunsell three-coach set (397) behind the tender, the engine made light work of it in open country between Downton and Alderbury junction. Stations on both the Salisbury and Brockenhurst routes east of Broadstone junction were closed from 4.5.64.

With pulsing exhaust echoing around the deep cutting, double-chimney Standard class 4 4–6–0 No. 75070 lifts its special excursion past Salisbury Tunnel junction on route for Southampton Docks on 20.3.66. During the 1980s the third side of the triangle, the Laverstock 'chord', has been re-instated and used for diversions. More recently it has served to turn preserved steam locomotives employed on special workings.

Some very imaginative enthusiasts' excursions were devised during the fifties and sixties, including one by the RCTS employing classic four-coupled 'fliers' from the past. The first stage of the tour on 14.8.60 was entrusted to former SECR class L 4–4–0 No. 31768. The gleaming engine covered the 83 miles from Waterloo to Salisbury in just over 90 minutes, seen approaching past the East Points ground-frame. Built by Beyer Peacock in 1914, No. 31768 was scrapped in 1961; there are no survivors of this type, nor its successor the L1 class.

When still less than six months old, the celebrated *Evening Star* 2–10–0 was rostered to take the 2.45 p.m. Portsmouth–Bristol (Temple Meads) service forward from Salisbury on 7.7.60. Almost always through services from Portsmouth or Brighton changed engines at Salisbury, so it was an ideal place to see a good cross-section of locomotives from both Southern and Western Regions. Class 9F No. 92220 was the final Standard steam locomotive to be constructed for British Railways, emerging from Swindon Works with copper-capped double chimney in March 1960.

Recalling *Mallard*'s visit to the Southern during the 1948 locomotive exchanges, class A4 4–6–2 No. 60024 *Kingfisher* ran a special train to Exeter on 27.3.66. The unmistakable wedge-shape of the Gresley streamlined Pacific, as well as its distinctive chime whistle, attracted many bystanders when *Kingfisher* rolled into the 'Down' main platform at Salisbury. Sadly, the locomotive was scrapped soon after.

Branch lines to Alton

The second of two special trains to mark the end of the S15 class in active service on the Southern Region coincided with a moderate snow fall in Hampshire. On 16.1.66 S15 4–6–0 No. 30837 was coupled ahead of U class Mogul No. 31639 for travelling 'over the alps' from Alton, the pair's exhaust muffled in the cutting approaching Medstead & Four Marks station. No. 30837 was equipped with a six-wheel tender for use on the Central Section.

After distinguishing itself earlier in the year, class L 4–4–0 No. 31768 was requested again for excursion work to power the LCGB 'South Western Limited' on 18.9.60. Still bearing a Nine Elms (70A) shed plate, the handsome 'Chatham' engine paused briefly at Alresford on the Mid-Hants route to Winchester, opposite the goods shed, before continuing its journey. Alresford closed with the remainder of the Mid-Hants route in February 1973, but re-opened as the western terminus of the Watercress line on 30.4.77.

A Sunday engineers' train was routed via the Mid-Hants line on 3.4.66. DMU operation had been introduced on regular Alton–Winchester City services in late 1957, but it was not until the 1960s that goods yards were closed and sidings lifted. While both Alresford and Medstead stations retained passing loops, the former looked bare after the sidings had gone. 'Crompton' D6506 in brunswick green livery waited to receive the token for the single line section through Itchen Abbas to Winchester junction, while Alton-bound unit 1121 swapped its token for the one to Medstead.

At Butts junction the Meon Valley and Mid-Hants routes diverged; in days gone by the light railway to Basingstoke had also parted company there. With the embankment carrying the Mid-Hants line just visible in the distance, class T9 4–4–0 No. 30337 ambled off along the Meon Valley with the 10.20 a.m. Alton–Fareham goods one fine spring day in 1953. The engine had returned to Guildford (70C) after overhaul at Eastleigh Works, and was very smartly turned out.

E.C. Griffith

Amid the wintry scene, class S15 4–6–0 No. 30837 took water at Alton on 16.1.66 while awaiting the arrival of 'Mogul' No. 31639, which had been running over the single line between Bentley and Bordon with the special train. From Alton, the two engines were to double-head the excursion over the steep gradients of the Mid-Hants. Note the old Southern Railway brake van in the goods yard beyond.

Bordon and the Longmoor Military Railway

Waiting hopefully for some incoming freight from BR, freshly repainted 0–6–0ST AD102 had steam up in the loop adjoining the LMR platform at Bordon on 10.1.66. The matching blue brake van was of the LNER design that was adopted as standard by BR. In the event, the BR goods from Bentley was cancelled, so the MoS saddle tank and brake trundled back to Longmoor without more ado.

LMR stations were always very basic, as the entire railway was intended for training rather than comfort. After its abortive trip to Bordon for interchange traffic, saddle tank AD102 paused alongside the platform at Oakhanger before continuing to Whitehill and Longmoor on 10.1.66. Notice the lamp hung over the drawhook and also that this particular 0–6–0ST was not fitted with vacuum brake to work passenger trains.

CIVILIANS EXCEPT WAR DEPARTMENT
EMPLOYEES ON DUTY, OR PROCEEDING
TO OR FROM THEIR WORK, MAY NOT
TRAVEL
SOLDIERS NOT ON DUTY, THEIR WIVES
AND FAMILIES, AND WAR DEPARTMENT
EMPLOYEES MAY TRAVEL AT THEIR
OWN RISK.

Cast notices displayed at important locations, such as Liss junction and Longmoor, spelled out who could – and could not – travel on the LMR. While a member of the Combined Cadet Force at college, the author travelled on the Longmoor system during the 1950s, and again in the course of public open days held annually in the sixties. The final open day was 5.7.69.

Author's collection

122

Although the LMR had quite a large number of wagons for internal use only, BR wagons also found their way onto the system at Liss and at Bordon. Some shock-absorbing open wagons were being shunted across a public road adjoining Apple Pie depot on the morning of 30.6.67, with 0–6–0ST AD199 performing with gusto. Perhaps as a consequence of being vacuum-fitted, this locomotive was painted blue and lined in red, lettering being in cream. Note duty disc 'D'.

On a murky 16.4.66, two of the MoS 0–6–0STs stand outside the depot at Longmoor. AD102 was an unfitted example, while WD118 *Brussels* had a number of non-standard fittings including being equipped as an oil-burner. Built by Hudswell Clarke of Leeds, this engine was originally numbered WD71505. Following preservation, WD118 found a home on the Keighley & Worth Valley Railway and remained as an oil-burner.

The oldest surviving Bulleid 'Light Pacific' that has not been rebuilt is *Blackmore Vale*. As SR No. 21C123 it was constructed at Brighton Works in 1946, renumbered 34023 under BR auspices and retained in traffic until 1967. Following preservation, it was stored at Longmoor for several years and steamed occasionally. On 20.7.68 it was simmering outside Longmoor shed between demonstrations. It is now kept on the Bluebell Railway.

Soon after 5 a.m. on the morning of 30.6.67, a plume of frothy steam marked the progress of 0–6–0ST No. 195 after collecting its single ex-BR non-corridor brake carriage from the depot at Longmoor. Engine and carriage then reversed across the road to Longmoor Downs station to form the ECS train to Liss junction. The high level track in the foreground was the route used.

Bulled-up in proper Army fashion, MoS 0–6–0ST No. 195 and brake compartment coach AD3031 stormed across the B2131 Greatham to Liphook road as the ECS train from Longmoor to Liss junction. Once there, it provided transport for the civilian employees at Longmoor Camp and any Army personnel who needed to travel. Duty disc 'A' was appropriate for this task. The date was 30.6.67.

On the morning of the final open day on the LMR, gleaming 2–10–0 AD600 *Gordon* swept majestically into Longmoor Downs with a mixed assortment of carriage stock – the leading vehicle was a former SECR 'Birdcage' brake in blue livery. The ungated level crossing on the right led to the yard, loco shed and depot, whereas the 'main line' from Liss crossed the same road on the level beyond the two-storey building.

Some impression of the sylvan nature of the terrain through which the LMR passed can be gained from this view of saddle tank No. 195 leaving Liss Forest Road station with a Longmoor Downs–Liss junction service on 30.6.67. The one-coach train provided transport for civilian employees at Longmoor and connected with BR trains at Liss.

Early one Friday morning in the summer of 1967 the empty stock to form the day's passenger train between Liss Junction and Longmoor Downs set off across the impressive viaduct above Longmoor Yard. Typical MoS 0–6–0ST No. 195 and an ex-BR compartment carriage, both in LMR blue livery, comprised the train. This was the final season of regular steam haulage on the system, after which diesels took over until closure on 31.10.69. Weavers Down forms the backdrop.

After arrival at Liss, 0–6–0ST No. 195 took water and began to run round its single carriage ready to form the next LMR service to Longmoor. Built by Hunslet in 1953, 195 spent its entire working life in Army service; it was withdrawn when regular steam haulage ceased on the Longmoor system late in 1967. This scene was recorded on Friday 30 June that year at about 6 a.m., just ten days before steam traction ended on BR (Southern Region).

The Portsmouth Direct line

The pick-up goods from Fratton to Guildford was still steam-hauled early in 1966. After shunting at Havant and Petersfield, class Q1 0–6–0 No. 33006 was busily engaged with coal wagons at Haslemere on 19.1.66, the snowy conditions prompting increased demand for household supplies. Within a couple of months this duty was taken over by the new series of ED (electro-diesel) locomotives and the last Bulleid 'Utility' withdrawn.

After the goods yard at Liphook was closed, the redundant signal-box and a semaphore Home signal were rescued for the Hollycombe Woodland Railway and Steam Fair in the grounds of
Hollycombe House, scarcely more than a mile from its former location. A short stretch of standard
gauge track has been laid, but the most ambitious contribution to the collection is a narrow gauge
line through dense woodland, of 1 ft 10³/₄ in gauge. In this view Barclay 0–4–0WT No. 1 *Caledonia*
holds centre stage while geared Aveling & Porter engine *Sir Vincent* and a Burrell road locomotive
flank it in a rustic setting; Liphook signal cabin is on the left.

Farewell to the 'Middy': after withdrawal of public passenger services the previous day, a final enthusiasts' special was organized by the RCTS for Sunday, 6.2.55. A pair of E5x 0–6–2Ts, Nos 32576 and 32570 coupled bunker to bunker, stopped at Midhurst with 'The Hampshireman' for a photo-call before continuing past Elsted and Rogate to Petersfield – the very last train of any kind to travel westward over the former LSWR branch. This picture records the reception at Midhurst, with people thronging the platform and even climbing the signal gantry to get a better view!

Chas White

With the frost lingering on railway sleepers, the 'Portsmouth Direct Line Centenarian' coasts into Petersfield station on 25.1.59. It was appropriate that the special brought a Drummond 'Black Motor' 0–6–0 (No. 30350) to this location, since Guildford-based examples of the class had appeared at Petersfield regularly in the past, not least on the Midhurst branch goods until 1951, when it was worked by ex-LBSCR designs from Horsham instead. The Midhurst bay platform was on the right, beyond the level crossing, while the old lower-quadrant semaphore signal was employed on those rare instances when push-pull operation was suspended, so that the engine had to run round its train in the electrified 'Down' main platform, or for freight movements.

After spending an hour or so shunting the 'Up' yard at Havant, class Q1 0–6–0 No. 33019 crosses over to the 'Down' line to continue to Fratton Yard with the 9.45 a.m. goods from Chichester on 14.10.58. In the foreground are the tracks connecting the main line to the Hayling branch.

With the strong evening sunlight reflecting off its polished boiler, the preserved Gresley Pacific No. 4472 (class A3, formerly 60103) *Flying Scotsman* draws up in Havant station with a return special from Salisbury to London (Victoria) on 17.9.66. Painted in LNER apple green, the famous engine looked and sounded magnificent; it is remarkable to think it has since travelled to America and Australia, but is once more performing in Britain, having been privately preserved after purchase from BR in 1963.

Hayling Island branch

Immediately on arrival at Havant from Hayling, the little class A1x 0–6–0T uncoupled and ran back to the buffer stop, there to take on water before running round its train in the bay platform. On 22.5.55 'Terrier' No. 32650 stood by the water crane with its Westinghouse air pump panting, while the fireman operated the point lever for the loop.

With safety valves lifting and steam in all directions, 'Terrier' No. 32650 conjures up a dramatic scene as it storms out of Havant with the 12.35 p.m. service to Hayling Island on 2.1.62. In the background a yard crane and goods wagons indicate some commercial activity; nowadays the land on either side of the main running lines is utilized for car-parks.

No separate freight trains were normally run on the Hayling branch. Instead, one passenger train in either direction was designated as 'mixed' and conveyed goods wagons attached to the passenger coaches as required. On 21.12.60 the 2.53 p.m. from Hayling came into Havant 'Down' main platform, with class A1x 0–6–0T No. 32661 hustling the assortment of stock over the miniature level crossing in lively fashion. This 'Terrier' retained the original small bunker and tool box as it had not spent time in the Isle of Wight.

With a few extra shovelfuls of coal on the fire, class A1x 0–6–0T No. 32650 darkens the sky over Langstone village while skirting the coastline towards the bridge with the 4.35 p.m. branch train from Havant to Hayling. A brisk south-westerly wind whips the smoke away from the long, tapering LBSCR chimney while the spark-arrestor fitted to all the regular Hayling Island 'Terriers' stands out against the clear sky. The date is 9.7.61.

In summer the railway had a distinct advantage over road traffic, for it had priority at Langston level crossing. While cars and buses queued on either side of the crossing, the little train swept in and continued on its journey after the briefest of stops. Class A1x 0–6–0T No. 32646 accelerated vigorously away from Langston past the twin-armed signal on a fine day in January 1962, in charge of the 11.35 a.m. Havant–Hayling service.

Another former Isle of Wight engine, 'Terrier' No. 32640, became a regular performer on the Hayling branch during the early 1950s and stayed to the end. On 1.5.60 it brought the 5.35 p.m. train to a stand at North Hayling, tickets being available from the guard. The variation in width between the two Maunsell carriages would indicate that the narrower example had been 'borrowed' from the Eastern Section. Note the LSWR B4-style chimney fitted to 32640.

In 1953 the former Lancing Carriage Works' shunter 515s was taken back into capital stock as No. 32650, being transferred to Fratton for use on the Hayling line. Soon after taking up its new duties, the little class A1x engine was pictured with an elderly LSWR corridor carriage approaching the main platform at Hayling Island terminus. At that time both platform starting signals were of LBSCR origin, mounted on timber posts, but the one in this view was later replaced by a SR upper-quadrant pattern when the wood became rotten. No. 32650 was preserved and now operates on the K&ESR line.

Lens of Sutton

On the last day of public services, 2.11.63, duties were shared by two octogenarian A1x 0–6–0Ts. Earlier in the day No. 32650 was in charge, but as the light began to fade No. 32662 came to Havant to lend a hand. Bearing a wreath around the base of the chimney, 'Terrier' 32662 whistled for Langston level crossing as it approached with the last Havant–Hayling Island service to run in daylight. The last public train of all ran with both engines and six carriages, the locomotives being marshalled at either end of the train to save running round: it was very late, very emotional and never to be forgotten.

Puffing vociferously at the rear of the five-coach special, class A1x 0–6–0T No. 32670 carried the headboard for the 'Hayling Farewell'. With brilliant black engines, green carriages, sunshine and steam galore, the Hayling Island railway took its final bow on 3.11.63. This was the scene in the cutting between Havant and Langston level crossing on the last journey to Hayling by BR train.

Hayling Finale On 3.11.63 a final special was run for the benefit of enthusiasts from London. A five-coach train was assembled in the bay platform at Havant to await the arrival of the excursion behind U class 2–6–0 No. 31791 via Fareham. At the head of the Hayling train stood the oldest of all the 'Terriers', built in 1872 as No. 72 but after successive renumberings it had become No. 32636. At the other end was No. 32670, the next Stroudley tank to have been constructed in 1872; the pair, at ninety-one years apiece, were the oldest working locomotives on British Railways.

Joint approach to Portsea Island

The 'Brighton' pierced the Hilsea Lines' defences in 1847, to be followed by the 'South Western' a year later, with tracks from Portcreek junction into Portsmouth being jointly owned until the Grouping. After the departure of the main Cardiff–Brighton through train from Fareham, the Portsmouth portion followed on behind once the section was clear. On 3.10.59 Fratton-based class M7 0–4–4T No. 30039 recalled its original express passenger role with the rear four carriages of the 12.50 p.m. from Cardiff as it bustled along between Fareham and Portchester, being due into Portsmouth & Southsea (Low Level) at 5.33 p.m.

Passing the site of the short-lived Paulsgrove Halt, 'Greyhound' T9 4–4–0 No. 30707 was in full flight with the 5.42 p.m. Portsmouth & Southsea–Basingstoke van train on 29.6.60. The halt had been opened in June 1933 to serve the racecourse (situated between the railway and the A27 Cosham to Portchester main road), but this closed with the advent of war in 1939 and never re-opened.

Obliged to pull out all the stops to grapple with the 1 in 283 out of Cosham, Drummond class 700 0–6–0 No. 30350 passed over Cow Lane bridge at a canter on 25.1.59. 'The Portsmouth Direct Line Centenarian' was heading for Gosport (via Fareham) with an interesting mixture of stock, including a Pullman, behind the tender.

With the winter sunlight glinting off the carriage windows, U class 'Mogul' No. 31801 plods uphill past the allotments west of Cosham with the 9.33 a.m. Portsmouth & Southsea–Cardiff General through train on 6.1.60. This service sometimes loaded to nine bogies (300 tons, tare) which was formidable for a mere 2–6–0 on such a difficult cross-country route; except in emergency, an engine change was scheduled at Salisbury where a WR 4–6–0 was the usual motive power.

The 5.45 p.m. Portsmouth & Southsea–Cardiff General service had eight bogies behind the tender on 13.9.57, when Standard class 4 2–6–0 No. 76067 brought the train of WR stock into Cosham. The main goods yard was on the left of the picture, but the cattle dock was on the opposite side of the line. The foot-bridge (known locally as 'Jacob's Ladder') is still there in the 1990s, but the goods yard and cattle dock have vanished.

Shuffling into one of the reception roads at Fratton Yard, class K 2–6–0 No. 32350 brings in the 10.03 a.m. Eastleigh goods on 17.2.60. To judge from the amount of steam escaping from the safety valves, the fireman might have been over-generous with coal during the latter part of the journey. Seventeen K class 'Moguls' were built for the LBSCR, but all the survivors were arbitrarily withdrawn in 1962; regrettably, none was saved.

In the pre-Christmas period, many additional trains were run by BR to help the Post Office clear the vast amount of extra mail and parcels. Some older suburban electric units were used, but this still left increased activity for steam too. One such duty was the 1.15 p.m. Fratton Yard–Eastleigh, a task entrusted to Standard class 5 4–6–0 No. 73086 *The Green Knight* on 23.12.59. With a Stewarts Lane (73A) shedplate, 73086 had a real assortment of stock in tow as it prepared to get under way.

While WR tender engines, especially 'Hall' class 4–6–0s, were seen at Portsmouth almost every weekday until 1961, the appearance of an 0–6–0PT was singularly rare. But pannier tank No. 4689 was allocated to 71G (Weymouth) and had just been given an overhaul at Eastleigh Works, so its arrival at Fratton on 22.12.60 was most likely part of the running-in process. Coupled to a bogie GUV and BR Standard brake, the stranger stood in the yard adjoining Goldsmith Avenue around 1 p.m. but later it was noted propelling empty carriage stock through the washing plant in the direction of Portsmouth & Southsea station.

Pre-Christmas mail and parcels trains offered a number of extra opportunities to see steam locomotives at work, sometimes at locations or over routes from which they had been absent for a long period. Some surprises could occur in the choice of motive power, too – for example, the 12.45 p.m. Portsmouth & Southsea–Brighton parcels duty on 23.12.59 was entrusted to veteran Billinton 0–6–2T No. 32515 of class E4, recorded passing Fratton with true Edwardian panache.

On the seafront within sight of Southsea Castle, a popular summer attraction for families was the Southsea Miniature Railway. The system had its own turntable and, in the fifties, two steam locomotives were available to work the trains. It was not usual to run both together, as each was perfectly capable of hauling the stock single-handed, but on 20.7.58 *Victory* and *Valiant* were spotted double-heading a well-filled train returning to the terminus by the paddling pool. After a spell with diesel traction and a simplified track, the SMR closed down before the new Sea Life Centre was constructed in the 1980s.

A newcomer to the Portsmouth area during the summer of 1959 was one of the Maunsell rebuilds of Chatham 4–4–0 designs of around the turn of the century. The particular engine that became common, following its allocation to Eastleigh, was class D1 No. 31735. On 10.7.59 it wheeled the 12.15 p.m. Portsmouth & Southsea–Plymouth through carriages along the cutting below Canal Walk; set 881 would be attached to the main train from Brighton at Fareham, for onward transmission behind a Bulleid Pacific.

When no superannuated 4–4–0 was available, the through carriages from Portsmouth to Cardiff or Plymouth were worked to Fareham by 0–6–0s, 2–6–0s or almost any other locomotive type that came to hand. On 7.7.61 the choice fell upon class Q1 0–6–0 No. 33037, which headed the 12.15 p.m. to Plymouth along the cutting towards Fratton with unmistakable sound effects. A Standard 4 2–6–0 on a parallel track was reversing towards Fratton MPD beneath Somers Road bridge.

Several journeys were made each weekday between Fratton Yard and HM Dockyard with stores and other materials for the Royal Navy. Until 1957 it was the routine to use an elderly 0–4–4T engine (latterly 02 No. 30207) because of the severe curve from Portsmouth & Southsea (High Level) round to Edinburgh Road level crossing. But after its withdrawal Fratton MPD started using a class E1 0–6–0T, or even a diesel shunter. On 26.8.57 the duty engine was the ex-LBSCR veteran, No. 32694, seen hurrying along the maze of tracks between Somers Road bridge and Portsmouth & Southsea station with the 1.57 p.m. from Fratton to Unicorn Gate and the Dockyard.

The regular weekday appearance of a Western Region locomotive at Portsmouth was varied on 29.2.56 when a 'Mogul' was rostered for the Reading train. 2–6–0 No. 6394 was coupled to Maunsell three-coach set 201 in platform 1 at Portsmouth & Southsea (Low Level) to form the 2.45 p.m. departure for Reading General in place of the more usual 4–6–0. This part of the Low Level station has been demolished and is now a car-park.

The relatively rare occurrence of snow on the south coast tended to disrupt the timetable in steam days much as it does today. On 15.1.60 Urie class S15 4–6–0 No. 30496 was despatched to get the through carriages for Plymouth as far as Fareham, and shuffled out of platform 2 at Portsmouth & Southsea (Low Level) as best it could not much after the official departure time of 12.15 p.m. There appeared to be no carriage heating available to passengers, but one could not expect everything. . . .

Through services between Portsmouth and Bristol or Cardiff offered most scope for steam locomotive crews to show off their prowess, as they were semi-fast and provided with very comfortable WR corridor stock. The 2.33 p.m. from the Low Level station to Bristol (Temple Meads) was especially challenging, since it was scheduled to run non-stop from Fratton to Southampton Central – one of the very few trains not booked to stop at Fareham. On 8.4.57 class U 2–6–0 No. 31792 of Yeovil (72C) was the engine, ready and waiting at platform 5.

Leaking steam beneath the footplate, the unkempt appearance of BR Standard class 4 2–6–0 No. 76064 was all too typical of the final days of steam power in the south. Forming the 12.15 p.m. to Plymouth and taking the coaches as far as Fareham, 76064 wheezed its way out of platform 4 at Portsmouth & Southsea (Low Level) on 17.2.66 – one of the few remaining passenger turns available for such an engine, which was barely more than ten years old at the time!

With the Royal Sailors' Rest on the opposite corner, the quaint two-arm signal at Edinburgh Road level crossing was one of the features of HM Dockyard branch from Portsmouth & Southsea (High Level) to Unicorn Gate. Originally, the two wooden arms were slotted into a timber post, but a redundant lattice post of metal construction was substituted in 1956. Goods traffic over this line into the Dockyard ceased during the 1970s and the track has since been removed. The signal post is in the care of Portsmouth City Museums.

Empty stock of the 'Luton Holiday Express' was retrieved from Portsmouth Harbour station on 28.7.59 by class E4 0–6–2T No. 32479, seen curving into platform 6 at Portsmouth & Southsea (High Level) at the head of LM Region corridor stock of Stanier design. The train engine had been S15 4–6–0 No. 30839. Note the mixed semaphore and colour light signal adjoining platform 7.

Special trains for enthusiasts to visit the 'working museum' railway system on the Isle of Wight were popular in the mid-sixties. The somewhat premature 'Vectis Farewell' of 3.10.65 – steam did not finish on the island until 31.12.66 – brought the oldest unrebuilt Bulleid Pacific to Portsmouth Harbour. An admiring throng was soon gathering around 'West Country' 4–6–2 No. 34002 *Salisbury* after it stopped near the buffers of platform 3; built at Brighton in 1945, it survived almost to the last days of steam in 1967.